Meaningful Conversations:

Connecting the DOT and True Colors®

Meaningful Conversations:

Connecting the DOT and True Colors.

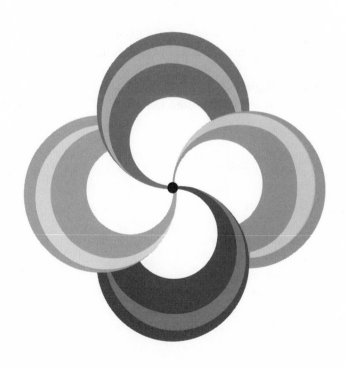

ANN KASHIWA

True Colors, Inc. Publishing
12395 Doherty Street
Riverside, CA 92503

TCB-050
Cover design: Chaunté Kashiwa and Cheri LeClear
                 Organic Ideas www.OrganicIdeas.net

Page layout: Sunrise Publishing, Orem, Utah
                 www.SunriseBooks.com

ISBN: 1-893320-26-X
Library of Congress Control Number: 2001089733

To my children

and

to my grandson

and

to the memory of my husband and parents

and

to all children worldwide.

My Thanks and Appreciation

Being connected to one's mentor for three decades is unusual in this fast-moving, ephemeral lifestyle to which we are accustomed. I take great pleasure in acknowledging my mentor and friend, Cliff Gillies, who has a special talent for fueling creative spirits to become the best they can become. Always available to discuss educational issues and to read and re-read manuscripts, Cliff has been my strongest advocate. I wish to also thank Sally Gillies for her sensitive and astute insights on human behavior and for her unmatchable hospitality.

My heartfelt thanks to my colleagues, Sharon and Wes Ruff, Steve Koepp, and Beverly Forslof, whose keen eyes picked up discrepancies and vague allusions and sharpened the focus of my message. They are my models for what a master teacher should look like. They are true professionals who have collectively invested 125 years in the education of the children. A special thanks to Bev and Sharon for their wise counseling, creative perspective, and many hours of meaningful conversations. Thanks also to my longtime friend, Betty Hughes, whose exacting comments on content and language helped me direct my attention to details and accuracy.

With her usual wit and acumen, my college classmate, Paulette "Pepper" Whitcomb from the G.W.U. days, critiqued several versions of the book. She squeezed my project in between her responsibilities as Editor-in-Chief of EnergyGate,

Petroleumplace.com. Also, a very appreciative bow to her daughter, Isabel Zimmerman, who critiqued the manuscript in its final stage. Her experience as counselor for the criminal justice and mental health systems was valuable.

Through the *True Colors* seminars, I was fortunate to connect with professionals representing Hawaii's higher education institutions. Their knowledge of *True Colors* and expertise in teaching, administration, and counseling heightened my awareness of different perceptions and perspectives. Laurie Toma Libarios, counselor, along with her father-in-law, Ernest Libarios, professor and counselor, at the Leeward Community College in Aiea, Oahu, viewed the manuscript from a counseling point of view. They are compassionate advisors to young adults, who are carving their niche in life. Denise Nakaoka, assistant faculty specialist and academic advisor, and Niki Labarios, academic advisor, at the College of Education at the University of Hawaii in Honolulu, also critiqued the manuscript from a counseling perspective in guiding future teachers. Their insightful comments helped me clarify the components of *The Dot* and *True Colors* into a coherent story. If it were not for Dr. Virgie Chattergy, I would not have met these professionals. As professor and Assistant Dean of Student Academic Services at the University of Hawaii College of Education, Virgie supported their training that incorporated *True Colors* into counseling. It was a pleasure to plumb the depths of her expansive experience and access her talent to analyze and synthesize.

I wish to express my very deep gratitude to the *True Colors* organization and its leadership. Don Lowry, the visionary founder of *True Colors,* is an ardent spokesperson for improving communication. His passion for *True Colors* is unwavering. John Butler, vice president and general manager of Educational Systems International (ESI), the publishing arm of *True Colors,* was an inspiration to me. His insightfulness, encouragement, and confidence in me kept me focused. As my editor, Larry Barkdull's sharp eye for details was extraordinary. He polished my writing and at the same time honored the intent of the content. I appreciate his ability to communicate in precise language and style. My thanks to Mike Berry, Mike Church, and Brian Carter for their artistic talents and technical expertise in transforming a manuscript into a book.

My children, Patti, Kent, and Jeff, and their spouses, Norman, Christine and Chaunté, have been involved from the beginning, reading and re-reading the manuscript from fragments to its entirety. Chaunté, with the assistance of her colleague, Cheri LeClear, was my art consultant in designing the cover and web site. My family's "go-for-it" attitude inspired me to finish this project. They were my cheerleaders.

—Ann Kashiwa
June 1, 2001

TABLE OF CONTENTS

Preface

MEANINGFUL CONVERSATIONS: CONNECTING THE DOT AND TRUE COLORS®

"Having a meaningful conversation with an adult" was the wish most often voiced by students at Mariner High School. A variation of that response was "Having a meaningful relationship with an adult." We asked students what they felt was most important to them, they responded, and we acted accordingly. Their candor and honesty guided us in creating a school climate in which all students felt special and could succeed. We began to identify elements of a successful school.

In 1970, Mariner High School was established as the first high school in the Mukilteo School District in Everett, Washington, sixteen miles from the northern boundary of Seattle. Located along the I-5 corridor at the edge of a rapidly growing metropolitan area, Everett retained its ruralism for two decades until the city limits spilled northward into the next county.

Mariner was one of thirty-six international Model School Projects, developed by Dr. J. Lloyd Trump and administered by the National Association of Secondary School Principals (NASSP). Mariner's vision was to create a high school with an elementary school climate wherein adults personally looked after and cared for each student. Mariner was considered to be on the cutting edge because of its innovative approach—its

Advisor-Advisee program, interdisciplinary and cross-disciplinary curriculum, team teaching, continuous progress, and non-graded report cards.

The Advisor-Advisee element embodied the spirit of the school. We met for twenty minutes twice a week for ice-breaking activities, four-year planning and registration, monitoring progress, and discussing any issue important to the advisees. If an advisee were called into the vice principal's office for disciplinary action, an advisor was also there as an advocate. The Advisor-Advisee group became a family with a mixture of ages and grades as well as a span of abilities and needs. We took field trips as a group, much like family outings. Upper classmen tended to take younger students under their wings. Advisors became personally connected to families and frequently participated in family celebrations during special occasions.

Our advisor-person idea extended to other students in our classrooms. Advisors learned to be counselors, not only to their advisees but also to other students in their classes. Therefore, many students had one official advisor and many surrogate advisors. The staff visualized an atmosphere in which meaningful conversations could become commonplace.

As a teacher and advisor, I interpreted "meaningful conversation" as dialogue that would touch a person's *center*, reflecting the core of that person.

Labeling this center as "the *Dot*," I defined it as the end point of philosophical questions such as, "Who am I? What am I? How do I fit into my world (high school environment) and the outside world (adult, work place)? And what makes me happy?"

As a parent and teacher, I have tried to listen to the children's voices and their silent spirits to help them touch their *Dots*. There is no single way to get to the *Dot*. It is a heuristic process whereby a student, through his own investigative techniques, gets to a truth about himself. This method is visibly demonstrated in such physical activities as sports. These activities, therefore, are aggressively encouraged in schools to help students bring together their diverse experiences, including academics, to reach their centers (*Dots*). Professional and Olympic-medal athletes refer to their *Dots* with terms like "my day," "being on," or "everything coming together."

However important the *Dot* concept is, there exists no curriculum to teach kids to get to it. Schools and homes provide a myriad of choices for children with the hope a child will connect with one and that eventually the child will catch on and get fired up. How often do we hear from teachers and parents about a child's "not living up to his potential"? There are far too many kids who are dissociated from learning and the school environment. They barely scratch their potential.

There are, on the other hand, an array of tools that can be taught to connect the student with learning. One strategy is the *True Colors* metaphor in helping a student understand "Who am I?" and "What I have to be to get to what I want to be." We all struggle with the "hafta bes" and "wanna bes" to get to "who we are" and "what we can become."

True Colors describes clusters of personality traits through four colors: Orange, Gold, Blue and Green. Everyone has attributes from all four colors, but it is his primary (dominant) color that gives each person his aura. The *True Colors* process helps students define who they are and how their personalities are reflected in their "colors." The subjects of social studies and literature were my vehicles to connect with my students.

Keeping notes on kids helped me to focus on the issues, mostly on *their* issues. I wanted to find out why I was successful with some students when I couldn't get through to others. What kept that group from learning and behaving as they should or wanted to? Something kept them from opening up to let knowledge in, and I, as a parent/teacher, didn't have enough strategies to reach them. This disturbed me. In reviewing the piles of notes and essays decades later, I discovered them to be about education, kids, teachers, and parents—how can we become better in teaching and learning? My husband and I started writing a book twenty-three years ago, but we never finished it. We were overloaded with responsibilities of parenting and preoccupied with professional advancement.

Stories about young folks who were mapping out their personal pathways touched me. *Everyone struggles* was confirmed to me. Because the stories of their journeys are more important than their names and races, I have made up names, in some instances to protect their privacy, and I have tried to make their races irrelevant to the issue. I wanted to emphasize that the stories are about teens and their hard or easy times. To this end, I have included many anecdotes throughout the book to highlight their struggles and triumphs. I have also used the pronoun "he" as a universal pronoun overriding gender. The "he/she" is awkward for me.

Everyone has a story to tell. While each is unique to that person and a particular circumstance, there are common threads that are recognizable. The struggles for both individuality and belonging are the same in Edmonds, Washington as they are in Destin, Florida. Balancing this dichotomy is part of growing up.

Three experiences in my life fast-forwarded me to another level of awareness. It was not so much a change in direction, as it was a deepening commitment to that same direction. The first event was the sudden loss of my spouse, a friend and confidant, on December 28, 1991. The other was an auto accident involving my daughter-in-law and myself in an unexpected blizzard on January 11, 1998. We could have been killed or permanently maimed. We were lucky. The third crisis had to do with health. One out of eight women are diagnosed with breast cancer. I was one. The prognosis was good, however. Thanks to state-of-the-art technology, an excellent team of experts in allopathic and complementary medicine, and loving family and friends, I am a survivor.

A brief postscript needs to be included here, just to illustrate an example of an unexpected coincidence that often occurs in life. Before my husband died, he had researched and perfected a solution for healing burns, skin abrasions, bee stings, and sore throats. By researching the common ingredients of natural healing remedies, such as aloe vera, Hawaiian grass, Chinese herbal tea, and cucumbers, he developed his Essence of Aloe.

Although he did not have an opportunity to market it, it has been the Number One healing solution for family members and friends. By saturating the radiated areas after my daily radiation treatment for six and one-half weeks, I avoided any sunburn or irritation to the skin. Little did my husband know in the 1980s that his tinkering in the lab would be crucial to my recovery twenty years later.

The sifting of information during these healing periods polished the lenses of my understanding and clarified my direction. I felt the urgency, not only in my life, but in the lives of today's young people and in the institutions that educate them. The search for answers permeates our nation. Each one of us defines what we are all about by trying to better ourselves and our society. We connect with each other by seeing how we are alike in the midst of diversity.

Meaningful Conversations is not meant to be an autobiography, although parts of it may seem so. Rather, it is a story about the learning, teaching, and growing up of everyday folks doing their day-by-day jobs. It is about ordinary people who don't give up. Finding happiness, or our *Dot,* seems to be a universal experience, and because of this, we span age, culture, and ethnicity. For me, to keep reaching, learning, and sharing, I needed to converse and to write. I feel I am in the right place at the right time.

Chapter 1

BECOMING A PARENT AND A TEACHER

Picture a six-year-old barefooted kid feeding pigs and chickens as part of her chores in a non-English-speaking immigrant family. There were no kindergartens then. Before she could enter the first grade, she had to be able to print her full name neatly on a line. She practiced and practiced, but *Tsuneko Murayama* kept falling off the pages; there were just too many letters in *Tsuneko*. She picked *Joyce* as her American name, but that didn't work either—too many letters. She settled on *Ann*, because it fit the page.

She spoke pidgin, a blend of Japanese and English, with a spattering of Hawaiian, Tagalog and Ilocano. She knew, though, that her teacher expected "good English" from her students. In the era of the World War II decade, speaking English well was synonymous with patriotism. *Ann* wasn't sure what good English sounded like. No one she knew spoke it. You might say she and her classmates were the original English-as-a-Second-Language (ESL) students in this plantation village school, surrounded by red dirt roads and sugar cane fields.

Pu'ukolii Elementary School graduated nine 8th graders, three girls and six boys. *Ann* wore new shoes for this occasion, and they blistered her feet. The date was June 8, 1948.

Cultural factors shaped me. From my Asian family, I inherited the respect for learning, as well as the value of effort, discipline, and loyalty. From the island environment in Hawaii,

I learned to mix play with hard work and to view the world in a multi-colored hue. The diversity in ethnicity, language, and culture instilled in me tolerance and an appreciation of my world's similarities and differences.

My later education and opportunities may seem a bit incongruous with this humble beginning, but it is an American story repeated many times over. It is about a child's dreams and successes made possible by riding on the backs of others. The greatest gift a teacher can give students is to fuel their dreams and teach them the skills, knowledge, and attitudes in order to achieve them. I was blessed with teachers who had strong backs. They hoisted me and inspired me to charge ahead. They reminded me that I could do more than I imagined. I wanted to be that kind of a teacher.

As a second generation American, I learned the history and dynamics of the United States, and I learned them so well that I began to teach teenagers what it is to be an American and what kinds of things we can do to align our actions with our ideals. Each year, I challenged my students with a hypothesis: "We are in the midst of a great human experiment. If this nation achieves unity through the celebration of its diversity, then we will have accomplished what no civilization has done. Is this the challenge for the new century?"

Historically, powerful nations have felt compelled to subdue those who were different to make them fit into the dominant culture. The evolution of this nation, however, has taken a different path. We are committed to the democratic principles of freedom, to the belief that all persons are indeed created equal, and that the purpose of government is to protect that freedom. Each generation attempts to use resources and institutions to correct injustices. This has become a tradition for many Americans. We continue to fight the good fight for equality, equity, and freedom for all, especially for those who are voiceless.

And how will they—the students—contribute to this end? The standing joke in my classes was that students will have to report back to me one day and tell me how they were bettering society. Many of them have. They update me on their dreams and accomplishments, as well as those of their schoolmates. For example, Mark practices medicine; Ivan, Dave and Becky practice law; Gaby and Mojuana are artists; Kyle and Gemini are in computer land; Pamela is assistant vice president and senior financial consultant for a major investment firm; and countless others are homemakers, teachers, counselors, nurses, executives, entrepreneurs, artisans, athletes, members of the Armed Forces, and on and on. I am grateful they passed my way and enriched my life. They have done me proud.

Learning and the drive to be good at something start long before a child steps across the threshold of a classroom. Those qualities *start at home*. Because parents are "the child's first and most important teachers," a partnership between home and school is a natural relationship. (Boyer, *Basic School*, p. 47.)

My husband and I knew that before our children went to school, they had to be ready emotionally, psychologically, and scholastically. They relied on our sustained support. We held back one of our children at kindergarten because we didn't feel that he was ready for the big jump into first grade. We considered many factors—his birthday in the fall, his being physically smaller than others and less focused on formal learning. This was a tough call for us then, in 1967. Today, it is common practice to start children in kindergarten after their sixth birthday.

We wanted to make sure that he didn't feel like a failure, so we boosted his confidence in other areas, such as judo and chess. We also concentrated on tutoring him ourselves in reading and writing. Years later, as a college senior, he exclaimed, "I'm the only person I know who flunked kindergarten!" Then, in his understated humor, he added, "Boy, that extra year of kindergarten sure made a difference." We all had a good laugh. The difference of one year is miniscule in the total picture of one's life. College graduates are all ages today. My husband and I made the right choice.

I was a stay-at-home mom for ten years and did not get my teaching certificate until my youngest child was a first grader. I always knew that I would be a teacher one day. My husband, who was a university teacher and researcher for dental and medical schools, was obsessed with understanding how the human heart and mind work in processing information—scientifically and philosophically. Studying philosophy was one of his avocations. I was more practical and wanted to put ideas to use. We looked to the writings of Ralph Waldo Emerson, Henry David Thoreau, Teilhart de Chardin, Karl Jaspers, T.D. and S. Suzuki, J. P. Sartre, Abraham Maslow, and Lawrence Kohlberg. They kept us searching for answers about our lives. Later, we reached for John Glasser, Deepak Chopra, Bill Moyers, and Joseph Campbell, to name a few.

Emerson's *Oversoul*, Teilhard de Chardin's *Omega*, Campbell's *Passion*, and Maslow's *Self Actualization* touch upon the universal centeredness of a person. They go beyond the trivia and minutia of daily living, often overriding human frailties. We coined this phenomenon the *Dot*, which is discussed in Chapter 3. This ineffable *Dot* is what a person is all about. It describes a state of mind and a glimmer of perfection that come from hours and hours of practice, resulting in the action becoming an indivisible part of the person.

In a materialistic world, young people often say they want to "make lots of money" or "get rich and retire young." This thinking represents the other end of the spectrum of the *Dot*. "Making money" is not necessarily bad, unless one is consumed by it. The recurring advice we gave our children was to "follow their passion" and the money (or fame) will follow. This means "giving it your all" and becoming good at your position. This applied to their school work, activities, hobbies, jobs, and career choices. A slight change in attitude can turn a mundane task into a challenge, a game. This change comes through a *twist* in perception.

I became a better teacher by first being a parent. I tried to communicate through my *Dot* to help students seek theirs. I accepted the good and the bad, as parents do, and I maintained a single-minded focus on what was good for each student. I reminded myself often that teaching was about the student, not about me. I saw the subjects of history and literature as vehicles to get the student to understand himself and his past and his current environment.

I also became a better parent by becoming a teacher. I became less demanding, less critical, and more accepting. Working with extreme diversity in every facet of education helped me gain a broader view of how my own children fit into their generation. Further, I gained a better balance between pushing them and knowing their range of abilities. I learned to appreciate and enjoy them.

Unlike many horror stories about raising teens, my husband's and my experience was nice. This is not to say that we did not experience exasperating moments and pain. Sometimes we wondered if the hospital had made a mistake in sending us home with the wrong child. "How can an offspring of ours be so moody, irritable, obnoxious...?" Of course, other parents experience similar sentiments, so we were not alone. Another interesting experience parents share is the interaction between family members: If one child is wearing horns for the day, his siblings behave perfectly; then they all take turns wearing horns.

For the most part, we viewed the teen years as real opportunities for us to walk the uneven terrains with our children as they moved toward adulthood. We struggled to teach the *Dot* to our children. We searched for ways to communicate effectively about attitude, perception, effort, and success. We didn't have a "sure fix."

I was introduced to *True Colors* in 1994. I was a senior counselor at a student leadership camp at Cispus, Washington, in the foothills of Mt. Rainier, when I first used *True Colors* with a group of student leaders. They found it interesting, however they did not apply the concepts to their lives. Four years later in 1998, I was re-introduced to *True Colors*. I was in a better position to appreciate the infinite ways that *True Colors* can be applied to improve communication, curriculum, teaching and parenting.

True Colors is a user-friendly personality assessment to help people communicate directly with their inner person and with each other. The colors represent a cluster of personality types—Orange (adventurers and doers), Gold (traditionalists and stabilizers), Blue (sympathizers and supporters), and Green (investigators and viewers).

True Colors is one of the most effective ways of getting to the *Dot*. An Orange may get to it through sports (performing); a Gold may get to it by creating or perfecting a system (organizing); a Blue may get to it through poetry (writing); and a Green may get to it by investigating an unknown (researching). *True Colors* expands our awareness of ourselves and others.

As adults we take on the responsibility to seek the best tools for communicating with ourselves and our children. Parents are teachers, whether or not they are certified, and teachers are parents whether or not they have children of their own. The common denominator is the focus on their missions: Both are in charge of another's growth and future. And they both need to care.

Chapter 2

ON PARENTING: HAVING A PHILOSOPHY AND A MISSION

As young, inexperienced parents, we muddled our way through the child-rearing decades from the late 1950s through the 1970s. We did it without the support of extended family nearby. Grandparents and close relatives were thousands of miles away. Our friends became surrogate families, linking us to an extensive support system. By surrounding ourselves with people we loved and trusted, we created a cushion for our kids.

Parents love their children and want them to be happy, well-adjusted adults. This statement is hardly controversial. But the way we love them can be controversial. Love is complex. There are many levels of love. It can be, in teen vernacular, "mush"— hugs, kisses, soft cooing words. It can also be tough love, saying no to a child when experience tells us that the long-range effect of his actions can be disastrous. Love is also nudging and coaxing a child to learn. It is about letting a child make mistakes or fail without guilt or shame, and about helping him problem solve. Love is about having faith to let him go off to explore and experiment, knowing that it is risky to allow him to discover the depths of what he is and can be.

Balancing the dichotomies—freedom vs. discipline, holding on vs. letting go, yes vs. no—is at the crux of many family problems. My husband and I viewed balancing as an art for which there were no guaranteed recipes for success. We followed our heads and hearts and paved our own walkways. The following are some ideas that worked with our family:

We tested our philosophy and beliefs. What were the forces behind our patterns of behavior? How deep was our commitment to this philosophy? Did we walk our talk? Applying the abstract to practice was challenging (Chapter 3). We knew we would impact the kinds of adults our children would become. As parents, we evolved to become our children's coaches, teachers, and mentors. They, in turn, taught us how to be decent human beings. And they taught us how to laugh at ourselves.

Our mission centered on building our children's character. We asked two questions:

1. What kinds of traits do we want our child to have?
2. What do we want to see in each child at 10? 15? 20? 40?

Convinced that an individual should be able to live with himself, we concentrated on having our children like who they were. Such people would tend to be kind, thoughtful, and able to stand firm. They would speak up against injustice. The anecdote below illustrates this point.

> The taunting was targeted at a disabled youngster on the school bus, "Retard, stupid...hey, do this now." Two boys told the tormentors "to knock it off" and "leave him alone; he didn't do anything to you." Friends of the two defenders joined in the protest. Peer pressure worked on a handful of bullies. The harassment stopped on the bus. The disabled

student and the two boys remained friends throughout elementary school.

If negativism is nipped in the bud, a situation does not have to escalate to crisis level. A person who is comfortable with himself need not manipulate, exploit, or put down others. Negative vibes deplete one's energy and contribute to disequilibrium and unhealthiness. My husband and I wanted healthy children.

We reinforced the value of hard work. We encouraged our children to jump life's hurdles and push the limits of their comfort zones. By urging them to stretch psychologically and physically, we hoped they would raise the bar themselves without our help.

> Stick-to-it-ness became our slogan. One of the projects we tackled was to cut into a 30-degree sloping backyard. Since no trucks or tractors could access it, we parents and children dug into it by hand, a little at a time. Passersby must have thought we had lost it. Many may have thought we were building a swimming pool—the hard way. The goal was clear—to level a section of the yard for a play court for the kids. The process became a game—measuring the progress, celebrating at certain benchmarks, treating ourselves to a movie or a burger-and-fries feast. We all learned that one can overcome physical discomfort and fatigue if the goals are clear, achievable, and if the process becomes teamwork. No task was considered too menial for any team member.

Taking responsibility for one's self was also valued as part of our family's mission statement. Responsibilities also extended to helping others. We believed in expressing our appreciation to those who preceded us, and to contribute to those who would follow. The gratitude expressed would balance out the self-absorbing "me first" attitude, which was prevalent among our children's generation.

In addition to developing a philosophy, we questioned our commitment to it. We had to be honest about our own goals, strengths, and fears. Our pattern of consistency would reflect how deeply we were committed to our beliefs. True commitment does not necessarily mean how unwavering we can be. Instead, it means how far we can stray from it without losing sight of it? How far can we explore and not get lost? We have to be flexible and open to examine a problem from all angles. If we were to be inflexible and dogmatic, we could find ourselves rearing youths who were angry and rebellious, or at the other end of the spectrum, fearful and spineless. Either type tends to be unhappy and therefore adds tension to a household. We struggled with this concept as we faced each problem and counseled each child.

In teaching children the value of "teaming" within a family, we consciously down-played the "me first" attitude. We also believed that children, who were considered to be "too precious" exhibited brattish behaviors, which we did not want in the family. A "too precious" child needs to be the center of attention all the time, has an inflated view of himself, always gets what he wants from adults and peers, and will pout or throw a tantrum when he is unhappy. Both the "me first" and "too precious" attitudes could handicap a child. By getting between a child and his ability to grow up and do things for himself, adults could actually stunt his growth.

> Colette, a 14-year-old freshman at a large high school in an affluent neighborhood, came in for a conference with her parents, who were both airline employees. Their high-profile jobs took them out-of-town often. The issue was Colette's absenteeism that could have caused her to lose credits in her classes, even though her grades were good. That her parents loved her was obvious; they did everything to make her happy. During the conference, she made excuses for her behavior, "talked back" to her parents, and generally did not take responsibility for her actions. Her parents had given her everything she wanted—a large clothing budget, a generous allowance, and a brand new car, which sat in the garage until she could get her driver's license two years hence. This crisis ended on a happy note, because the student, parents, and school worked together. The possibility of failing 9th grade scared Colette. To begin, a tighter structure was set up for Colette to function within the acceptable boundaries of home and school. Parents planned for quality time with their daughter. As experience shows, it is the quality, not quantity, of time spent that opens up communication. While this example of a "too precious" child is one from an affluent family, my experience has shown me that this attitude prevails across socio-economic lines.

Poor parent-child relationships can result in a boomerang effect. Whatever one teaches a child, consciously or unconsciously, comes back to us. A child, who is allowed to be self-centered and manipulative, will continue in this direction unless there is a conscious attempt to change those patterns. In the formative years, a child may camouflage these anti-social behaviors from his parents. Eventually the behavior will be directed at the parents. The aggressive, manipulative child may turn into a rebellious, angry teenager, ready to confront an equally angry parent. When either party has had enough, the child may storm out of the house or be thrown out, frequently after an "either-or" confrontation. Since patterns of effective communication had never been established, the parent and child cannot return to a time when dialogue was open and honest. Instead, they must pioneer new paths. Sometimes an outsider, such as a counselor, can ease the process.

A crisis often forces better communication. As a high school assistant principal, I found myself in the middle of many tense family situations. My goals were simple: (1) To deal with the student's infraction and make sure parent(s) and student understand the rationale for the consequences; (2) To have the student and parents articulate what they could do to improve the student's behavior and to move on to a more productive pattern of behavior at school and at home; and (3) What does all this have to do with the student's future?

> Julius, a junior, was in my office for fighting with another student. This would have typically brought an automatic suspension from school. Another fight would have resulted in a long-term suspension for the remainder of the school year. Julius was a former dropout, then he had enrolled in an alternative school, and in his junior year, he had transferred to our high school because he wanted "a regular high school diploma."
>
> He was agitated that morning about how his life was going. He and his mother were not getting along. He had moved out of the apartment four days before and was bunking with friends. "She hates me," he confided. "She took my

bedroom door off and it pissed me off so I packed up and left." That was the last straw in his mind.

Mom was powerful in her language and demeanor, a no-nonsense constituent, whom the office staff knew well. In my phone conversation with her, I learned that she took the door off because Julius had lied to her about having friends and alcohol in his bedroom. He had violated her trust, so she got mad and took action. In telling me his troubles, he left out the alcohol part. I shared with Julius' mom his perception, that she didn't love him and was constantly on his case. She was stunned that he thought she didn't love him.

During his three-day suspension from school, I recommended they go to a Burger King, have a coke, and just talk. Here was a young man with so much potential. Good looks and charm to boot. Upon his return to school, Julius told me that his mom had treated him to a dinner at a fine restaurant and they had talked through dessert and beyond. He had returned home and the door was back on its hinges. "It sure beats Burger King, huh?" was my comment, to which he just smiled and nodded. He never got into trouble again.

An addendum: In late spring, I received a call from Julius' mother, who was obviously frightened and speaking at a rapid pace. Julius had worked hard to stay straight and to distance himself from his ex-gang friends. His mother said, "They're going to hurt my boy." She shipped him out-of-state to live with relatives. We prepared an official transcript packet that she could send to his new school. She kept the location a secret. I want to believe he received his "regular high school diploma." He, himself, was motivated and had a mom who wouldn't give up.

Crossfires between parent and child are exacerbated by inadequate communication skills. Fuses are shorter and tempers are higher when life doesn't seem to be going right. Perceptions polarize. A parent views the child as ungrateful, selfish, mouthy, demanding, and lacking respect. A teen, on the other hand, says his parent never stops yelling at him about doing this or that. He views his parent as hypocritical. Teens tell me they hate hypocrisy in their peers and in adults—saying one thing (i.e., belief in freedom and individuality) while doing another (i.e., putting down people who think and behave differently). This double-edged value system, they believe, breeds intolerance, narrow-mindedness, and distrust.

How can communication lines remain open throughout the phases of childhood and parental development? Both parent and child are growing and changing. For one thing, an adult can stop telling a child what to do and how to feel. This is obviously easier said than done.

The following are concepts that my husband and I taught, repeated, reinforced, and rewarded. These concepts kept our pathway lit. We tried to eliminate the blocks along the way. We followed a simple formula that our children could grasp.

Positive energy + Hope = Healthy person

Mission

Keep the mission simple. Ours was "a person has to be able to live with himself and take responsibility for his own well-being." When something went wrong, like getting a D on an exam, it was easy to blame the test, the teacher, other kids who raised the average. The challenge was in changing our children's attitude to look within themselves—accept what they did or did not do, and recognize how to change the process, and expect different results. Keep the rules simple and at a minimum. That will make monitoring less stressful. Too many *Do's* and *Don'ts* complicate the mission, and besides, who wants to keep track of the scoreboard?

Goals

Help a child set realistic goals, breaking them down into bite sizes. Each benchmark has to be doable. Unrealistic expectations can be a problem. Living up to parents' expectations can become a heavy burden for a child, especially if his capacity or interest is not similar to those of his parents. A child will stop trying, and is often labeled an underachiever. He will do the minimum, just short of failing. If expectations exceed a child's comfort zone, he will rebel by not trying at all, for if he doesn't try then he can't possibly fail. On the other hand, underestimating a child is equally harmful, for he grows up believing he is a loser. "What I do doesn't matter. Why should I even try?" Fear of failure is a heavy damper on learning.

Effort

Effort becomes a habit, but in order for that effort to make sense, an adult has to reinforce and remind the child that effort pays off, extrinsically and intrinsically. Receiving positive feedback and being truly appreciated are the Number One emotional needs of every person. With appreciation comes respect, self-worth, confidence, and esteem.

Confidence

Help the child develop confidence and self-esteem and he will learn to be at ease with himself, be honest, and accept who he is.

In order for children to accept who they are, we adults need to accept who they are, not just verbally, but in our daily actions. Everyone can learn, and I am convinced that everyone has at least one talent.

Expertise

Help a child become an expert at something—anything. Little accomplishments build confidence. The expertise need not be newsworthy or of importance to anyone except the child and his parent. It need not be competitive. But this accomplishment should demand discipline and effort from the child, so that he feels the task is worth his while. The expertise will encourage him to stretch his talent and energy. He has to feel good about his product and about himself: "I did it!"

Transferring

Help him transfer this feeling of success to other tasks, acting as reminders to the child that he indeed can do other things. Give him phrases like, "Remember when you did...?" There should be many, many "remember whens..." As a high school teacher and administrator, I was saddened to hear that a parent's last recall of "remember when" occurred during his child's second grade year. That child was now an 11th grader. Were there no other "remember whens" in between? Positive reinforcement is critical in a child's early years. He internalizes the gratification of a job well done and it becomes a habit. We never lose the need for positive reinforcement. We like to be acknowledged and appreciated for a job well done, or for simply being ourselves.

Having fun

A balanced life includes laughter and fun. Fun is defined differently by each family through the arts, recreation, sports, and hobbies. Every region in the U.S. provides countless outdoor adventures and cultural outlets; some are pricey but many are free. One of our family's favorite activities was tenting across the state and exploring the wonders of each area.

When the winter freeze came, we transformed our neighbor's patio into an ice rink. We two moms and our five children all piled into a station wagon and cruised through every thrift store within a five-mile radius, until everyone had his own pair of ice skates. The makeshift ice skating patio-rink congealed the neighborhood and brought hours of pleasure.

At another time, our family, along with two other families, hiked into the Snoqualmie National Forest to select a Christmas tree. The permit cost two dollars. After twenty minutes of hiking, the kids decided to play in the snow with their sleds. The moms and dads went searching for that perfect tree. As they walked deeper into the forest, the dads sank in snow up to their waists while the moms stood on top of a hill directing their husbands to the best spots. They found three beautiful trees and the kids loved the sledding. And the picnic lunch was the best. But the next day, our husbands came down with bronchitis for having been wet and chilled chasing the perfect tree. The following year, the three families bought their trees from the Boy Scouts and never went back to playing Paul Bunyan. The children, now all adults, glow as they laugh about those adventures as the best part of growing up in a close-knit community.

Children have open minds to try something new and are quick to learn. One parental responsibility is to teach children to use their leisure time productively. It is food for the mind and heart.

Family structures today are more complex than they were even a generation ago. Many factors contribute to this dilemma (Chapters 6 and 7). Frequent mobility, for example, dislodges stability. A network of extended family is rare. Single parents are the norm. Two working parents add pressure to the structure. Blended families or living arrangements, which combine children from different marriages, tax everyone's communication skills and patience. Emotional chords are taut. Stress levels are high. Therefore, the role of parents, as parent-teacher-coach, is more challenging than ever. The more knowledge and skills people have in their repertoire, the more successful they will be in their relationships. The conversations have to keep on going.

Chapter 3

ON PARENTING:
FROM ABSTRACT TO PRACTICAL

Being a Professional: Experiencing the Dot

My husband and I searched for tangible examples to convey an intangible message to our children, who were reaching out to get in touch with who they were and who they wanted to become. From our experiences, we discovered a metaphor that we believed captured the "centeredness." We called it the *Dot*. The symbol (•) and the word *Dot* seem neutral and do not carry emotional connotations that other words do, such as heart, center, soul. There is no exact location of the *Dot* within us. It is a place where our physical, mental, and emotional energies come together.

To get to the *Dot*, we coined the phase, "being a professional." The term professional was to communicate unity, that "gotcha" feeling. It is becoming "professional" when one experiences riding a bicycle, being totally balanced, with no hands. It is the automatic stage that follows hours of practice—working through the do's and don'ts, learning the art of balancing, not overcorrecting, feeling abrupt change in direction, zigzagging, falling, scraping shins, then learning to balance tentatively, all the while picking up enough speed to maintain the balance. Finally, riding a bike is no longer cerebral; it is internalized (at a subconscious level) so one doesn't have to think about it. The coordination is mastered and the rider is "a professional."

Another example is the multiplication table, a handwritten table posted on the wall of the dining room, which for us became the eating, lounging, studying, and gathering place. The dining room was the room where everyone congregated before, during, and after dinner. It was located in the architectural and social center of the house. The dining room was conveniently situated next to the kitchen with a pass-through counter between the two rooms.

Learning the posted multiplication tables became a game to see how fast the children could respond to the numbers that were called out— "9x5, 8x6, 4x3...." The hesitant responses became smoother the more we practiced. The times tables were internalized and the responses became spontaneous. Again, reinforcement, praise for improvement, and the goal to be "a professional" in multiplication cemented their skills with numbers. Thus, if we found that a child understands the concept of being a professional (riding a bike, understanding multiplication, etc.), then the same notion can be transferred to other activities.

A DIAGRAM OF THE *DOT THEORY*

Adapted from Herbert K. Kashiwa, Ph.D., 1965, Louisville, KY

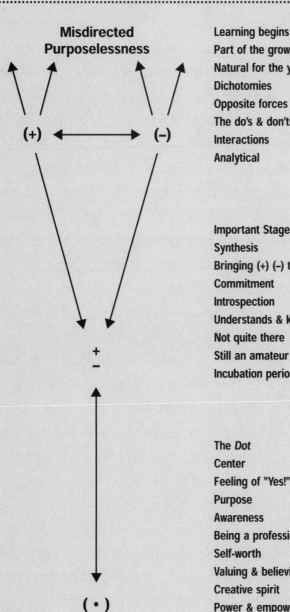

Misdirected Purposelessness

(+) ⟷ (−)

Learning begins
Part of the growing process
Natural for the young to be here
Dichotomies
Opposite forces
The do's & don'ts
Interactions
Analytical

+
−

Important Stage: Intentional
Synthesis
Bringing (+) (−) together
Commitment
Introspection
Understands & knows
Not quite there
Still an amateur
Incubation period

(•)

The *Dot*
Center
Feeling of "Yes!"
Purpose
Awareness
Being a professional
Self-worth
Valuing & believing in self
Creative spirit
Power & empowerment

It is a simple diagram that our children could visualize and grasp. The *Dot* could be experienced by them at an early age. Parents often marvel at the naturalness and spontaneity of their children. Children act from the *Dot*. Children don't necessarily know how to recreate it or get to it at will; the *Dot* is just natural. As one matures, the activities and depth of the *Dot* become more sophisticated. In an attempt to grasp life's complexities, we try to organize and simplify. And in simplifying we clarify the complex.

Paradoxically, a natural inclination of children to react from the *Dot* is not enough for personal growth. It's a hit-and-miss phenomenon without conscious effort and practice. By gathering and testing our knowledge and skills (+) and (-), the hard work, practice, and concentration to get to ($\pm$) is a learned process. I interpret Joseph Campbell's "Quest" in the ($\pm$) range. It represents a stage of a hero's journey to self-awareness and enlightenment (•).

The *Dot* or the Center is an elusive concept, for it really lacks a definitive term. The Dot seems to be tied to all the good things. Qualitative descriptors, like "happiness" and "fulfillment," are intangible. These are valuative terms to measure the quality of life. Although most of us feel the *Dot's* presence, there is a vagueness connected to describing it.

Dr. Caroline Myss's "personal powers" dwell in the *Dot*. Like Myss, Gary Zukav's writings center on a person's spiritual side. In differentiating between the personality and the soul of an individual, he walks us through the evolutionary process of tapping into one's soul. The soul evolves through responsible choices one makes that may or may not lead the person toward the "Light."

The *Dot* is that part of a person that expresses a basic truth about that individual. The *Dot* is enveloped in self-worth, the way we value ourselves. It is honest, simple, and beautiful. It radiates unity and balance, oneness and harmony, order and freedom. It is the unencumbered quality by which we can honestly communicate with others and with ourselves.

Behavior that emanates from the *Dot* is, I believe, a universal quality. Most of us have experienced this phenomenon in small ways. An excellent cook, for example, is excellent because he has mastered the minute, often disorganized details, and simplified the procedures so that all behavior becomes a sum of his experiences. Athletes and artists, in particular, seek to perform from their *Dot*. The sum of their experiences is based on unglamorous hours of training and study. They have internalized their experiences to make their behavior appear effortless to an onlooker. Those who have mastered their skills exceptionally well are usually labeled talented or gifted.

When we observe a superb Olympic gymnast, for example, we appreciate his harmony, balance and oneness, because he is performing at his new level of consciousness. He has mastered the art of the sport and performs from a force within his *Dot*. He is indeed a professional, an artist.

At age 24 Tiger Woods is a phenomenon. Hailed as golf's epitome of athleticism, he abandoned the swing that won him many tournaments and in an effort to improve, created a new swing. In the August 24, 2000 edition of *Time* magazine, he remembered the buckets and buckets of balls that he went through to practice his new swing. It took him countless hours for a whole year. *Time* journalist Dan Goodgame describes, "Then suddenly, on one swing, he sensed—for the first time in a year—that he had done exactly what he had been trying to accomplish." "Pure shot" was what Woods was after, and, what seemed to be fleeting moments of perfection, he now experiences on command. He appears to be operating within his *Dot* because he becomes better and better.

Another golfer, Chris DiMarco, who won the PGA SEI Pennsylvania Classic in September 2000, credited his success to the feeling that it was "his week" and that he was "connected to every bounce, every tree…"

The 2000 Summer Olympics in Sydney, Australia showcased superb athletes who also seemed to have been performing from their *Dots*. Misty Hyman described her Gold medal moment: as she walked out to the starting platform, she felt she was "in my zone" and "completely at peace" to win the 200-meter Butterfly. Another swimmer, 16-year-old Megan Quann from Puyallup, Washington, won two Gold medals: one in the 100-meter breaststroke, and another as a member of a relay team. Coming from behind, Laura Wilkinson of Texas won a Gold in diving: "I went all out on that…I didn't hold anything back." A journalist described Michael Johnson's running style as "a work of art" as he ran for his fifth Gold medal in a relay. I imagine that the Athletes Village housed athletes who vowed to give it their all *(Dot),* whether they medalled or not.

Like the body, the mind too has to practice—thinking. "To shoot baskets well one needs to practice. To think well one needs to practice. Going to school is practicing to use one's mind well." (Sizer, *Horace's School*, p. 25)

As a parent and a teacher, I am interested in tapping into and awakening the unglamorous 85% of talent.

> Paul was a champion swimmer headed for the state tournament that would prompt a scholarship. He was self-assured, sometimes bordering on arrogance. He did not see how the subject of U.S. History had anything to do with his future, and he performed at a passable level, definitely below his potential. My telling him how important history is did not convince him. I had to speak through his Dot in the area of swimming.
>
> I asked him to describe how he felt when he won, not about his strokes and speed, just how he felt at that moment. He had difficulty at first, but when he described "that feeling," we transferred it to his academic performance. It took several conversations to make the connection between swimming and history. He ended up with a strong B and a better attitude. He went on to win a state title, and received a scholarship to a university.

The *Dot* is an identifiable experience that is ephemeral and fleeting. The paradox of the *Dot* is the permanence of the concept and the impermanence of its application. If we feel the *Dot* and try to dwell in it, we lose it. It immediately becomes the (+) or (-), and we have to begin the process all over.

One doesn't live in the *Dot*; however, a small number of people, like Mother Teresa and His Holiness The Dalai Lama, appear to do so. Each religion can list individuals whom they believe lived through the *Dot* and have shown others how to seek it. Sometimes we have to be still, listen, reflect, and be patient.

Recognizing and mastering this process takes training and hard work. Gaining mastery by means of the academic route is the most challenging. Why even attempt it? Because of our commitment to humanity and our development as citizens of this world and this nation, we need to raise the consciousness of human ideals and support policies and institutions that celebrate human dignity.

My husband's and my goal at home and at school has been to help our children transfer tangible experiences (athletics, art, cooking, bicycle riding) to intangible experiences such as learning, personal growth, and human relationships. Authority comes from within (Suzuki, *Zen Mind, Beginner's Mind*). Recycling these skills sounds so very easy. Not! It takes half a lifetime or more. Why?

Getting Lost Along the Way

The connections and transfers of experiences do not happen through osmosis. It takes coaching and counseling. Some people are not aware, or don't care, while others run from themselves. The postponement is merely a decoy, for they will have to deal with themselves one day. Getting lost along the way does not have to be a permanent situation because there are many ways to get back into the driver's seat and take control. We always have a choice.

Fear keeps us from nourishing the *Dot*. Fear controls behavior and drains the energy. A person's ability to build elaborate hidden agendas surpasses his ability to dismantle the very structure that keeps him from resolving conflicts. We want to protect ourselves from hurt and rejection. We often weave a complex web to protect our egos, so that we cannot find what is hidden. We also wear blinders that shut out any clue that might point to an enlightened view of ourselves. As the web becomes more tangled and complex, we expend energy and time on focusing on the web, rather than on repairing and strengthening our *Dot*. The longer we avoid getting in touch with ourselves, the higher the risk of emotional and physical burnout.

While many are distracted and try to escape, others are distracted by tackling conflicts head on. Confrontation may be a good way to deal with conflict, but confrontation without reaching for the center, the *Dot,* creates an even deeper schism. The "you-me, them-us" dichotomy gets nowhere because no one wins, not even the winner. If this pattern continues, the issue may become forever dichotomized, and thus irresolvable.

Confrontational or adversarial relationships are often resolved through compromise, so that the focus is on the nature of the compromises (i.e., establishing guidelines for rewards and punishments or monitoring agreements) rather than on the causes of the conflict. We look for practical, short-term answers instead of understanding the causes. Too many dead-ended endeavors anesthetize an individual's sensitivity as he seeks to find himself. On the other hand, living on a perpetual collision course traumatizes individual self-esteem and confidence.

An alarming number of people try to get in touch with themselves through drugs and alcohol, which is nothing short of attempting a shortcut to the *Dot*. This practice, however, has an enormous price tag. Their temporary euphoria, which to them is synonymous with happiness, leads them further away from the *Dot* and to their inevitable physical and emotional destruction. The ripple effect from addiction flows throughout the family and society. Addiction stunts one's growth in all areas and eventually it destroys the person and those around him.

A dysfunctional human being is costly to himself and to society. The escalation of crises among the young is epidemic. The dependencies on chemical substances; the incredible numbers of victims of psychological and physical abuse; the runaways, who congregate in urban centers and become victims of predators, or become predators themselves; and the high percentage of teenage depression and suicides. All these are indicators of malfunctioning societal relationships.

Parents and Teachers with Goals

The *Dot* can be targeted from any direction. Each person carves his own pathways, depending upon his life experiences and his quests. It takes a conscious effort to teach an individual how to seek the *Dot*. That effort starts at home. The broader the foundation, which parents build for the child, the easier the learning process becomes for that child.

A classic Japanese children's toy is a bright red plastic doll called *daruma*. Designed like a punching bag without arms or legs, the *daruma* always returns to its upright position no matter how hard you try to knock it over. It has a broad weighted foundation. Like the *daruma*, we need to broaden and weight the experience base of the child. No matter how many punches he experiences in life, he will always be able to return to his center of gravity. If there is a sound and consistent philosophy operating within the family, knowing how to prioritize becomes a natural part of growing up.

Fear is one of the realities of life. Acknowledging, accepting and incorporating healthy fear into one's life helps build self-worth. Moreover, if a lifestyle is mired in inconsistencies, the message transmitted to the child is naturally mixed. The child must learn to decipher the hidden agenda of the parents, and his energies will be expended on guessing what the real agenda is. The child would likely feel inadequate, dumb, or helpless because he cannot outguess his parents. Furthermore, he learns to develop his own hidden agenda and manipulates others to suit himself. This feeds into his instinct to survive, which is pretty strong.

On the other hand, schools should help the student decipher, interpret, prioritize, regroup, and incorporate information into a useful body of knowledge. The interplay of the emotional and psychological makeup of the student, during this process, is important because it fuels his retention of knowledge. Because the learning process is repetitive, one would think practice makes perfect, but this is not necessarily so.

The key word is prevention. We should teach people to act before a crisis arises, to anticipate problems, to visualize a sequence of events under various conditions. In other words, we should teach people to first study the alternatives and examine the consequences in resolving an issue, and secondly to take control and act. As conflicts and crises are common life experiences, it would be less threatening to look at other people, i.e., examine historical personalities and issues. Let us learn from the past before applying the process to ourselves.

A history teacher, like a parent, must have his own agenda. What is the bottom line? I believe it is to teach the process of inquiry through acquisition and interpretation of knowledge and skills, as well as inquiry into issues and self. Needless to say, the inquiry is a two-way interaction. The "self" refers to both the student and the teacher, for the teacher most likely learns more about himself and about history than does the student. The knowledge of history is the medium, the vehicle. My ultimate goal for students was to give them a healthy knowledge and appreciation of the past and a hope for the future. This goal, I concluded, would be measured by a student's ability to critique his own emotions and motivations through evaluating what he had done, what he can do, and what he would like to do.

The teacher-student time is precious because of the limitations of class periods and the school year. Therefore, the teacher has to cut out the fluff and get to the core as quickly as possible. That means eliminating the games and trivial rules and regulations—all those items that hinder honest human interactions and dialogues. The teacher has to recognize many *Dots* as quickly as possible, but in order to maximize the relationship, he has to have a strong clue as to where his own *Dot* is.

Ideally, a student should have sighted a glimmer of his *Dot* by the time he graduates. He should be able to point to who he is, what makes him happy, and he should be able to demonstrate an activity that he is mastering to help these goals "come together." It is through the *Dot* that he can reach out for intimacy in human relationships, professional growth, and where he may contribute creatively. This does not happen magically. It is a learned skill.

April 12, 1983. A sophomore class on Jazz Improvisation at the Berkelee College of Music in Boston. Jeff connected the *Dot* by perfecting a musical note, a phrase, in his practice sessions. He titled his speech on the subject, "A Mountain and a *Dot*." The speech described the process of his learning from a Boy Scout adventure—an eight-day hike into the Cascade Mountains in Washington State. The weather was foul, the terrain unmanageable, and trails overgrown. The consensus of the troop was that the hike was not as fun as previous hikes. Their goal was to jump-start this experience, get to the top as fast as they could.

Jeff's "beginner's" mind left him without the preconception of what a fun hike was supposed to be. Being the only novice and the youngest hiker at age fourteen, he viewed everything as new. He concentrated on the process: "Step-by-step, taking care of business day-by-day, just doing and enjoying." In retrospect, he concluded that there was a difference between "having a clear goal and not living the goal." His beginner's mind interpreted the weather, terrain, and trails as parts of the total experience. The awesome territorial view from the peak rewarded his struggle of getting there.

He felt the pleasure of the *Dot* on the top of the mountain. To him, the exhilaration he remembered about that experience was repeated many times over, as he mastered a musical piece, connecting that perfect note to that perfect phrase.

Chapter 4

WHAT COLOR IS YOUR CHILD?

I wish I had known about True Colors when I was in high school. I would have understood why I never felt like I fit in with other kids. I thought it was me, that I was weird or something. I didn't think I could talk to anyone at school about what I was feeling and thinking. I liked studying and making good grades. My parents told me college would be different. It was. I loved it. I found others like me.

A Green Child

This sentiment was expressed by my very Green daughter, whose positive academic experiences in high school revolved around two teachers. One was her art/ceramics teacher and the other was her Advanced Placement English teacher. In these classes she found other kids focused on art, ideas, and their futures. She felt safe.

Greens make up only twelve to fifteen percent of the population, and of those, thirty percent are female. She was in a minority in more than one way—in her ethnicity and personality. Statistically, female Greens represent only three to five out of every one hundred students. Out of her graduating class of

467, we could predict seventeen to twenty-five Green females. Lonely? Out of place? You bet—not quite connected with the high school agenda of after-game dances, parties, dating, jobs, cars, and cruising around. A Green would not necessarily fit into the social atmosphere of any typical high school.

Greens think in terms of concepts, vision, the big picture, complexity, nonconformity, and challenges. Greens appreciate intelligence and independence, and often, Greens are energized by working alone or with a small team of like minds. Small talk and social functions are not their forte. Thus, academic challenges appeal to Greens.

For a parent of a Green female, you need to be supportive. Home should be a haven, a safe place to retreat when necessary. Security in the family and excelling in academics will bring esteem to that child. Individual athletic prowess, such as downhill skiing and tennis strengthens esteem. Artistic pursuits—drawing, sketching, ceramics, pottery—polish the edges.

As adults, Greens often pursue careers in mathematics and science. Greens are known to mull things over, analyze, and not make snap judgments. My Green daughter married another Green after a long fourteen-year courtship. They were both focused on their respective educations and careers in health science. Today, she has a successful dental practice. Their family includes a toddler and two beagles, all three exhibiting varying shades of Orange. Husband and wife are voracious readers, whose curiosity crosses over several spectra of knowledge. They are quiet, enjoy a small group of friends, and pursue physical outdoor activities—biking, jogging, downhill and cross country skiing, backpacking into the wilderness, and kayaking through the isolated islands off Vancouver Island in Canada. These Green-Orange type activities help a person hover around the *Dot*.

An Orange Child

Already a charmer at sixteen months, our Orange child loved our neighbor "Dot-Dot" (for Dorothy) because she always had a cookie ready for him when he knocked at her back door every morning after breakfast. Rain or shine, this ritual continued until he found other playmates his age who were more entertaining. But, having appointed herself as his guardian, Dot-Dot continued to be his cookie queen.

School was a blast. It was the social scene that got him up excitedly every day. His kindergarten teacher, by contrast, handled things otherwise. Though an experienced and highly reputable teacher, Mrs. P. called a parent meeting because this class puzzled her. She was having difficulty in keeping control of a class in which boys outnumbered girls three to one. Her kindergarteners were energetic, extroverted leader types. The time-out corner was occupied every minute, I'm sure. Our son spent his share of time there, and our dinner conversations revolved around why he had been sent there and what he could do to prevent this. Our five-year-old did not really see the time-out corner as a punishment, rather just another playhouse.

Oranges are gregarious talkers and doers, especially the extroverted ones, and they need to be physical. They are good with tools and gadgets. They thrive in an exciting environment with lots of challenges, and if the environment is considered boring, they will invent excitement with whatever tools are available. They make up thirty-five to forty percent of the adult population. One finds Oranges in school among the performers, athletes, and student leaders; their charismatic personalities make them natural leaders.

Elementary school years: My husband's and my goal was to slow down our son and help him focus. Scouting was one big play time with many outdoor challenges and social interactions. Downhill skiing was a challenge in concentration and coordination. He begged for a unicycle after he saw children on TV riding them. Since no one he knew owned one, he would be unique.

We combed the bike shops of the entire city and finally found a Schwinn unicyle. Our son practiced in our hallway, banged up the walls and himself, knocked down door bells, photos, thermostats, and whatever was in the way. We dared not be in his route. Even our dog and cats knew better. He succeeded. In a few weeks he was riding in the neighborhood, to the shopping center, to school. The unicycle experience was one of the keys that taught him to focus, concentrate, and perform. And have fun. That's important to an Orange.

Performing was in his heart. Being on stage energized him, raised his esteem. In a community production of *Snow White* he was a proud eight-year-old "Grumpy." Today, he draws his energy from performing, composing, and teaching. He is a jazz saxophonist who performs locally, nationally, and internationally. He expresses his love for music through his *Dot*.

A Gold Child

Gold, the primary color of another of our children was less defined, more muted, sometimes projecting conflicting signals. As a Gold, he stayed close to home and family, saved money, loved the challenge of making money over the spending of it. He was hardworking, honest, and intensely loyal to friends. A strong sense of right and wrong anchored his behavior. He was pragmatic and practical. Even his education and eventual careers reflected traditional Gold. He majored in HRT (Hotel, Restaurant, Travel) and minored in business and accounting. He worked as an assistant manager at a popular restaurant, was a night auditor at a major hotel, and was a real estate agent.

Organization and precision, on the other hand, were not his obvious traits, as they are in most Golds. He sought different activities and got things done at his own pace and time frame. Being shy and introverted, he drew little attention to himself and "walked to the beat of a different drummer." He had many Orange characteristics, some of which he did not recognize or acknowledge until his adulthood.

He dreamed of becoming an entrepreneur, even before he knew how to spell the word. His first enterprise was a worm farm, housed in a large box-like bin that he seeded with earthworms. The worms must have liked their boxy hand-constructed condo because they fattened and multiplied many times over. He never took them to market; instead, he went fishing often, or gave them away to friends, or sold them to Dad.

He was intrigued with taking risks—in the stock market, poker with friends, the horse tracks. Although his bets were penny ante, he was successful and/or lucky.

His early jobs seemed to be more Orange than Gold. He spent two summers during his college years working on a salmon-processing barge in the rough Alaskan waters. This was a kid who suffered from motion sickness, and he chose to live on a barge for two-and-a-half months. The money was good, but conditions were risky—frigid temperatures, many fourteen-hour days, and flailing knives scraping against the fish scales, much like the Ginza knife commercial. In his second season, he was a salmon sorter, identifying the various fish by the shape and color of their tails—then tossing the chinooks and cohos into the correct bins.

Today, he sees himself as Gold-Green, and his persona reflects this. On the other hand, much of his behavior seems to draw upon his Orange. After analyzing his *True Colors*, he acknowledged his Orange. Oranges are most often identified with extroverted personalities, like many famous athletes and performers. Not all Oranges are extroverted, however. He, like countless other introverts, exhibits Orange traits that he tends to dismiss. It was a challenge indeed to meld his hands-on, restless Orange side with his Gold career choices in the areas of accounting and real estate. His Blueness is reflected in his deep compassion for others, and especially for animals. He now works to connect his *Dot* through the varied experiences he has had, from karate and chess to business and computers. His dream of becoming an entrepreneur is still alive. His deeply Gold-Blue wife helps him balance his dreams.

Mixed signals (from blended colors) are probably more common than we think. A child could give off conflicting signals, particularly if that child is a combination of Gold-Orange or Blue-Green. These colors represent contradicting traits, such as the steadfastness of a Gold vs. the impulsiveness of an Orange, or the sensitivity of a Blue vs. the aloofness and independence of a Green. These combinations seem to be opposites, but need not necessarily be at war. They simply reinforce the depth and complexity of a person's *True Colors* spectrum. No one is just Gold or Orange or Blue or Green; each is a blend of colors. While a person's spectrum may remain the same, the intensity of each of his colors changes with the situation. One needs to reflect and think about what he truly is.

Reconciling and balancing contrasting traits within an individual is a tough job. Empowerment through the *Dot* comes from integrating these traits. First, it takes recognition and awareness, then a plan for changing and strengthening certain patterns of behavior (habits). Parents need to step in, because they are their child's first coach and teacher. The child must not be alone.

A Blue Child

I have to look outside my biological family for an example of a Blue child. The child I am thinking about dreamt of becoming a dancer and an artist early in her life. She was a dreamer who loved being on stage. She was sensitive, intuitive, and articulate. Being sensitive, she took criticism to heart and took a long time to get over the hurt.

As a child, she was an artist who loved singing, dancing, and play-acting. Her grandmother, whom she considers to have been her "soul playmate," was an important influence. The grandmother loved and accepted this child with no strings attached, and supported her big dreams of being a singer, a dancer, an actress. In the child's early years, she auditioned for and received parts in school and community plays. Her favorites were musicals.

She was happy when she dressed up and performed for her parents' friends, or before a single audience, her grandmother. Her greatest joy, however, was performing at recitals. She loved the costumes with glitter and sequins, pretty ballet slippers, make-up and lipstick, and shiny things in her hair. The *Cinderella* ballet was a smash hit. For a seven-year-old, this was show biz. A somewhat shy child, she lost her shyness when she danced.

As an adult, she took more ballet lessons, which fulfilled her desire to relive the excitement she had felt as a child. She was also connected to the entertainment world. She now designs web sites for musicians and truly sees issues from her clients' points of view. Artistic flair in interior decorating is evident throughout her home. Her other job is sales for a high-end cosmetic company. What she likes best about this job is her role in helping people with skin care and general health. She connects with people through her heart and knowledge, and derives a sense of unity from her *Dot*.

Hindsight is Always 100% Better

I know my husband and I would have been better coaches and teachers to our children had we known about the *True Colors* metaphor. Our direction would have been clearer from the beginning and certainly would have enhanced our communication skills. *True Colors* would have given us a common language and a stable framework from which we could have spoken to our kids about behaviors, habits, goals, and dreams. The alternative hit-or-miss, trial-and-error system is okay, but using it takes much longer to get to the heart of a problem.

Parents' role—Keeping it Simple and Doable

Four words pinpoint a parent's role in helping a child grow to be a focused, productive, happy individual:
- Hear [Understand]
- Talk [Articulate]
- Walk [Guide]
- Laugh [Humor]

Hear: Know where the child is coming from, listen and hear. Our love may sometimes become overbearing as we project our own biases in molding or interpreting behavior.

Talk: Discuss in a give-and-take atmosphere. Exchange thoughts and feelings openly, without a scripted agenda or a top-down dialogue.

Walk them through. Establish clear directions and goals, breaking each down into small, achievable segments, and coach children in mastering each benchmark. Parents often tell their kids, "You can be anything you want to be." And they make it sound easy, like all one has to do is to want it badly enough. I worked with a 10th grader, Jason, who was convinced he was going to make it to the NBA. I asked him how he was preparing himself. He was cutting classes, failing his electives, and getting into fights. His position as a guard was tenuous, playing only a few minutes each game on the Junior Varsity team. He did not see the connection between his behavior and his dream. Parents sometimes neglect to tell their children how tough it can be. But the road need not be burdensome. It all comes down to taking small steps. An ample sprinkling of love, support, and encouragement from parents anchor a child's faith in himself when things go roughly.

Laugh: Indeed, life is serious, but if we take ourselves too seriously, we can become caught up in our own egos. We need to lighten up. People are funny with their idiosyncrasies and foibles. Laughter and humor buoy the human spirit and open up new perspectives in ways we view life and ourselves. Something that seems impossible can become possible just with a shift in our perception.

Doing True Colors Together

As public dialogue continues on education and what is best for kids, many young people are failing to connect with their school and their community. Some get lost in the shuffle. *True Colors* is one tool that can help people connect to each other and particularly to their dreams.

Finding your *True Colors* can become a family event. *True Colors* begins the process of self-discovery in a fun way. The process is user-friendly for both children and adults. The depth of discovery varies according to an individual's experience in life and how motivated one is to understand self and others.

There are several instruments that help one identify his *True Colors* spectrum. *What Color Are You?* is an outline that walks you through the process, step-by-step. The three sets of cards are appropriate for adults, students, and primary age. The *Advanced Word Cluster*, recommended for adults, and the *Word Cluster*, recommended for students, demonstrate how intense your colors are. The *Personal Profile* helps one color in the *True Colors* on a graph and to identify his strengths, joys, values, needs, and stresses. It also points to specific areas of needed improvement.

Children enjoy profiling (coloring) their family members. The *Family Profile* can often point to why one connects easily with a certain person and why he has to work harder to relate to another. The *Worksheet for Parent(s) and Child* helps a child see where each of them is coming from and how everyone can better communicate. It also helps students focus on who they are and where they want to go.

Enjoy.

WHAT COLOR ARE YOU?
Finding your colors and how bright they are

Card Sort

Choose one of the three sets of cards appropriate to your age.

1. Sort the cards by looking at the pictures.

   Place the card most like you on the left.

   Place the card least like you on the right.

   Determine your second most like you and your third.

2. Sort the cards by reading the descriptions of traits.

   Turn the cards over and read the descriptions.

   Place the descriptions most like you on the left.

   Place the descriptions least like you on the right.

   Place your second and third cards appropriately.

3. Choose one of the two Word Clusters, according to age appropriateness: (1) Word Cluster for intermediate through high school, (2) Advanced Word Cluster for high school through adults.

   Place the numerical value of each card on your Word Cluster.

   Write   #4—the one most like you.

   #3—next most like you.

   #2—next most like you.

   #1—the one least like you

Word Sort or Word Cluster

5. There are five rows of clusters. Take one row at a time.

   Reading across, place #4 on the cluster that is most like you.

   Place #3 on the cluster that is secondary.

Place #2 on your third color.

Place #1 on the cluster that is least like you.

6. Add up each column, including the numbers from #3 above (Card sort).

Twenty-four is the maximum number of points in each column.

The minimum points possible are six.

Determine your *True Colors* spectrum, from the dominant to the least.

If there is a tie in the points, let the placement of the cards determine your final spectrum.

Your Primary Color and the Brightness of Your Colors

7. The column with the most points represents your PRIMARY COLOR.

Second highest points represent your SECONDARY COLOR.

Third highest points represent your THIRD COLOR.

Fourth is the color that is least like you.

8. The point spread indicates how bright or faint your colors are.

Your Profile and That of Your Family

9. Visual display of your profile: color your colors on the Profile page.

ADVANCED WORD CLUSTER

Place #4 for most like you; #3 for next like you; #2 for next like you; and #1 for least like you.

Spontaneous	Responsible	Compassionate	Conceptual

ACTIVE OPPORTUNISTIC SPONTANEOUS	PARENTAL TRADITIONAL RESPONSIBLE	AUTHENTIC HARMONIOUS COMPASSIONATE	VERSATILE INVENTIVE COMPETENT

COMPETITIVE IMPETUOUS IMPACTFUL	PRACTICAL SENSIBLE DEPENDABLE	UNIQUE EMPATHETIC COMMUNICATIVE	CURIOUS CONCEPTUAL KNOWLEDGEABLE

REALISTIC OPEN MINDED ADVENTURESOME	LOYAL CONSERVATIVE ORGANIZED	DEVOTED WARM POETIC	THEORETICAL SEEKING INGENIOUS

DARING IMPULSIVE FUN	CONCERNED PROCEDURAL COOPERATIVE	TENDER INSPIRATIONAL DRAMATIC	DETERMINED COMPLEX COMPOSED

EXCITING COURAGEOUS SKILLFUL	ORDERLY CONVENTIONAL CARING	VIVACIOUS AFFECTIONATE SYMPATHETIC	PHILOSOPHICAL PRINCIPLED RATIONAL

TOTAL ORANGE	TOTAL GOLD	TOTAL BLUE	TOTAL GREEN

WORD CLUSTER

Place #4 for most like you; #3 for next like you; #2 for next like you; and #1 for least like you.

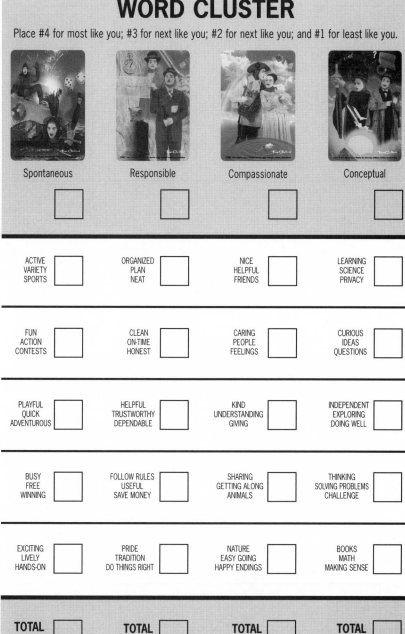

Spontaneous	Responsible	Compassionate	Conceptual

ACTIVE VARIETY SPORTS	ORGANIZED PLAN NEAT	NICE HELPFUL FRIENDS	LEARNING SCIENCE PRIVACY

FUN ACTION CONTESTS	CLEAN ON-TIME HONEST	CARING PEOPLE FEELINGS	CURIOUS IDEAS QUESTIONS

PLAYFUL QUICK ADVENTUROUS	HELPFUL TRUSTWORTHY DEPENDABLE	KIND UNDERSTANDING GIVING	INDEPENDENT EXPLORING DOING WELL

BUSY FREE WINNING	FOLLOW RULES USEFUL SAVE MONEY	SHARING GETTING ALONG ANIMALS	THINKING SOLVING PROBLEMS CHALLENGE

EXCITING LIVELY HANDS-ON	PRIDE TRADITION DO THINGS RIGHT	NATURE EASY GOING HAPPY ENDINGS	BOOKS MATH MAKING SENSE

TOTAL ORANGE	TOTAL GOLD	TOTAL BLUE	TOTAL GREEN

PERSONAL PROFILE • Flying Color Your True Colors

My name _____

These are my strengths: _____

I am happy when I: _____

I value: _____

I am stressed when: _____

My faintest color(s) is: _____

I would like to work on: _____

TRUE COLORS

Points	1st	2nd	3rd	4th
24				
23				
22				
21				
20				
19				
18				
17				
16				
15				
14				
13				
12				
11				
10				
9				
8				
7				
6				
5				
4				
3				
2				
1				

My brightest (primary) color is:

FAMILY PROFILE • Color Your *True Colors*

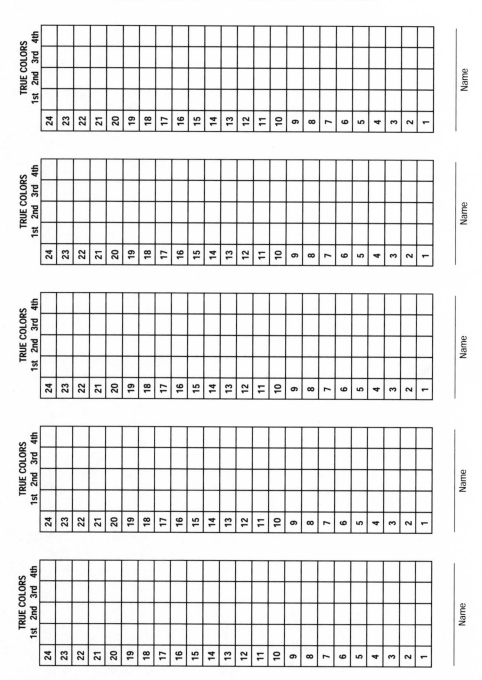

WORKSHEET FOR PARENTS AND CHILD

Parent: I believe in _____

_____

_____

Parent: My colors are _____   My child's colors are _____

_____   _____

_____   _____

_____   _____

Child: My dream(s) is to become _____

_____

Child: What I have to do to reach my dream _____

_____

_____

FOR THE CHILD

	At Home	At School
I'm very good at		
I'm okay at		
I need to work harder at		
I want to learn how to		

Chapter 5

FLYING ONE'S TRUE COLORS®

Making the Connections

Talkative, gregarious, street-smart, and intimidating to those who didn't know him well, Terry quickly moved into a leadership role among students who were vying for dominance on an urban high school campus. As a 10th-grade transfer from another state, he found his niche easily. His high energy, restlessness, and intense personality overshadowed his innate curiosity and intelligence. He spoke his mind, was argumentative with peers and adults, and often behaved impulsively. When he was happy, he gave bear hugs even to an assistant principal, who had days before disciplined him for truancy. His grades didn't reflect his intelligence or his potential. By 11th grade, he was barely passing his classes, falling behind in credits for graduation, and mixing with a tough crowd, whose modes of entertainment were rumored to include drugs, alcohol, and sex. Finally, his long discipline record and failing grades were too much for him. Terry dropped out of school. He became a statistic.

I would have guessed Terry's *True Colors* to be Orange-Blue, based on his behavior pattern. Terry and many other Oranges are among the underachievers who are often scheduled into special classes, such as a resource class. Sometimes evaluations are based on behavior rather than on academic potential. Because many of these students have not learned the basics, they are behind in their academic achievements. They are often below grade level in reading, writing, and arithmetic. A large number of students get tired of struggling and just give up. They become our disrupters and dropouts. Because they are restless and seek hands-on activities, the traditional classroom setting, with rows of seats and worksheet assignments, causes them stress. At the same time, their misbehaviors and failures cause stress to parents and teachers.

Statistics on failure reinforce this observation. According to a 1998 *True Colors* research survey of 14,000 students and adults on motivation and academic achievement, over fifty-one percent of all failures were in the primary Orange-Blue group. Of the students in the study, sixteen percent were Greens, fifteen percent Blues, thirty-four percent Oranges, and thirty-five percent Golds. For instance, if given one hundred students, the grade distribution looks like this:

SCHOOL GRADES BY PRIMARY COLORS

Compiled by Cliff Gillies, 1999, based on *True Colors* research

A's	11 Greens	9 Blues	4 Golds	0 Orange	(24)
B's	23 Golds	5 Blues	4 Greens	1 Orange	(33)
C's	18 Oranges	6 Golds	1 Blue	0 Green	(25)
D's & F's	15 Oranges	2 Golds	1 Green	0 Blue	(18)

Other statistics on at-risk students, from Canada and a Washington State middle school, substantiate the need for immediate intervention to help those students in the lower quartile.

Students in the lower quadrant are potential dropouts. They lose faith in themselves and in the system. Occasionally we read about or hear of dropouts who later turn themselves around as adults and become models to others. However, the reality seems to be that dropouts enter the adult workplace without adequate academic, social, or emotional skills. If the patterns of failure continue, their lives will be filled with struggle.

As a parent, a teacher, or an administrator, how would one go about reaching the "Terrys" before they become dropout statistics? Those connected with the real Terry cared about him. His mother agonized about his future and wanted Terry to succeed in earning a diploma and to get on with his life. Many of his teachers tried to help him. He did not hear what we were saying. He did not understand our warnings, and an interpersonal connection wasn't made. Terry missed his opportunity for success. I believe *True Colors* could have helped him understand himself and his environment. *True Colors* is a tool that can help people connect to each other and particularly to their dreams.

PRIMARY TRUE COLORS AND AT-RISK STUDENTS

Comparisons worth attention and concern

CANADIAN TRUE COLORS SEMINAR STATISTICS

Percentage of students' primary color

Student Population	Blue	Gold	Green	Orange
At-Risk (266)	29.3%	12.0%	10.2%	48.5%
Grades 7-12 (2271)	30.2%	28.1%	15.5%	26.2%
University (360)	32.2%	20.0%	20.8%	27.0%
Grade 8 (170)	28.2%	17.6%	15.9%	38.3%

A WASHINGTON STATE MIDDLE SCHOOL AT-RISK CLASS

At-Risk Students (25)	12%	8%	12%	68%

Notes:

1. In Canadian schools nearly half (48.5%) of the at-risk student population comes from about one-fourth of the regular school population (26.2% Orange).
2. The general populations of Canadian grades 7-12 and university students created a similar "spectrum profile."
3. Are teaching styles adjusting to "Orange" learning styles?

Sources: March 1999 report to a Washington State middle school and a Fall 1998 Canadian True Colors report. A compilation by Cliff Gillies and Ann Kashiwa.

A Process

The value of *True Colors* is in its simplicity and reliability. As a practical, non-threatening, and entertaining communication tool, *True Colors* focuses on respect, worthiness, and self-esteem for our personal and professional success. *True Colors* opens doors to better understanding and appreciating ourselves and others. The *True Colors* process is especially useful in communicating at home and at school. The dialogue continues, and meaningful conversations prevail between parent and child, teacher and student, staff and staff. Overall, *True Colors* generates a positive climate for learning and expands the teachable moments.

Based on the research of psychological types as defined by Carl Jung, David Keirsey, Katherine Briggs, and Isabel Briggs-Myers, *True Colors* was created by Don Lowry in the 1970s. *True Colors* was initially used by private institutions, and parents and educators have come to recognize its enormous applications to teaching and learning. Its beauty is in its simplicity, in enabling anyone to grasp the concepts. We tend to not forget our colors. Even third graders can understand and apply the concepts. Moreover, the process is non-threatening, self-revealing, and just plain fun. It opens up conversation and keeps dialogue moving along toward a greater understanding of "who I am." There are no right or wrong answers, no judgment calls; it is a personal revelation.

True Colors is a process for identifying our brightest and faintest colors in communicating our strengths, joys, values, and needs, as well as our stressors. Each individual determines what color he is. There is no authority figure telling someone what that person is or ought to be. We can clarify the differences between "Wanna be" and "Hafta be," in order to reach "who I am" and "what I want to become."

True Colors is based on the assumption that an individual has a primary color. The focal point, however, is that individuals are made up of all four colors, what makes an individual unique is the order and intensity of the colors. *True Colors* shows how he bonds to other human beings.

Each color is linked to a cluster of character traits.

> • The Spontaneous ORANGE represents energy, power, spontaneity.
> • The Responsible GOLD represents strength, stability, organization.
> • The Conceptual GREEN represents persistence, determination, challenge.
> • The Compassionate BLUE represents harmony, relationships, idealism.

It Begins with Me

We are all teachers, whether or not we are trained and degreed professional educators. Additionally, we are all learners, and know the process continues throughout our lifetimes. Therefore, teaching originates with insight into ourselves. Teaching begins with "me" since **I** cannot begin to impact others until **I** can understand myself. We teachers should be in touch with ourselves first before we can deal with others. By identifying *our* colors, we hold some answers to who we are and how to be in touch with our Centers (discussed in Chapter 3).

Who we are as parents defines the kind of environment we create at home and sets the tone within the family. Who we are as educators determines how content and skills are delivered in the classroom. And who we are as individuals weaves the delicate threads among human beings. Our awareness of ourselves and of others heightens communications, and we begin to view others and problem solve from a different perspective. Improved communication promotes peace and harmony.

The True Colors Spectrum— Oranges, Golds, Blues, Greens

The four colors represent four distinct clusters of personality traits. They represent a spectrum, because everyone has the four colors within them and can draw from each color to solve a problem or to appreciate life. The following examples will help differentiate one color from the other.

Oranges

Oranges see themselves as risk-taking adventurers, who like various physical activities. Orange represents energy, spontaneity, and action. Oranges wish to participate and live life to the fullest. Oranges are in the present tense. They are attracted to competitive sports, performing arts, sales, marketing, advertising, or any hands-on occupation. According to research by

True Colors, thirty-five to forty percent of the American population are primary Orange. A primary Orange has many others with whom to seek adventure and excitement.

We enjoy the company of Oranges for their spirit and spontaneity. The personality of a flamboyant, dramatic middle school art and ceramics teacher in a traditional suburban school would stand out. Schools are mostly run by Golds and Blues and the very structure of the school itself has Gold overtones—bells, schedules, details of classes, grades, field trip forms, supply and book inventories. However essential these details are, an Orange teacher would view them as nuisances and may overlook them, which could raise a red flag. Following through with details and paper work would not be her strong suit.

Oranges avoid conditions that would cause stress, such as:

   Being stuck at a desk
   Inactivity
   Lack of freedom
   Cornered by rules and regulations
   Following detailed instructions
   Inflexibility
   Inability to negotiate

On the other hand, Oranges are most cooperative when they:

   Can participate
   Can be given brief directions
   Can use tools
   Can be a star performer

Are allowed to promote ideas and activities

Can get immediate feedback

Famous people perceived to be Oranges are:

Franklin D. Roosevelt

Florence Griffith-Joyner

Michael Jordan

Marilyn Monroe

Elvis Presley

Ronald Reagan

Tom Cruise

Golds

Golds stand for convention, tradition, order, and common sense. Golds represent family, loyalty, dependability, and responsibility. They represent strength and duty, especially for the family. We depend on them for their organizational skills and details. Golds are efficient and task-oriented. They are attracted to administration, management, finance, accounting, and teaching. Golds, too, make up thirty-five to forty percent of the population. Thus combined, seventy to eighty percent of the population are Oranges and Golds.

Poor communication between a very Gold parent and a deep Orange daughter are common. It would be a stretch for the daughter to meet parental expectations—being steadfast, organized, predictable, dependable, and spending time with family. If she is unable to meet these standards, the Gold parent's perception of her might be that she is irresponsible, flaky, a goof-off, and disobedient, while the daughter might see her parent as autocratic, bossy, inflexible, boring, and old-fashioned. What steps could they take to repair the damaged communication lines and to realign their perceptions of each other?

Golds avoid being in an environment that is:

Disorganized and chaotic

Unfocused, lacking in direction

Too loose and offers too much freedom

Lacking in leadership and goals

Sloppy

Inconsistent

Ill defined in the responsibilities of each team member

Golds, however, are most cooperative when they are:

Recognized and acknowledged for their contribution
and hard work

Allowed to complete a task

Given clear and specific directions

Comfortable with rules that are consistent

Sure that what they are doing is right and ethical

Part of a team that is productive

Famous people perceived to be Golds are:

George Bush

Connie Chung

Walter Cronkite

Queen Elizabeth

Henry Ford

Billy Graham

Nancy Reagan

Blues

Blues illustrate romance, love, and compassion. Blues are naturals in making friends quickly. They relate positively to others and are quick to give support. They are the peacemakers, the harmonious members of a group or family. They are insightful and bring out the best in people. They are communicative and poetic. We look to them as mediators.

Blues are attracted to careers in counseling, nursing, training, human resources, and other people-oriented institutions. Primary Blues make up twelve to fifteen percent of the population, seventy percent being females and thirty percent males. Of the twelve to fifteen Blues out of every one hundred people, eight to ten are females and three to five are males.

In September, a Blue male student is scheduled into a 6th period high school U.S. History class, which is made up of mostly football players, wrestlers, and a few girls from choir and drama. As a parent, how would you support your son to have a positive high school experience? As a teacher, what strategies would you need to create in order for your students to interact respectfully with each other? How would you create a sense of belonging in the family?

Blues are stressed in environments that reflect:

Disharmony and conflict

Coldness, lacking warmth and caring

Isolation or being ignored

Negative remarks

Insincerity, lying, backstabbing

Routine, detailed work, and deadlines

Placing system or paperwork before people

Blues thrive when they are:

Encouraged by others

Expressing how they feel

Involved in people issues

Creative

Humanistic

Impacting others

Famous people perceived to be Blues are:

Julie Andrews

Princess Diana

Michael Jackson

Carl Jung

Richard Simmons

Mother Teresa

Oprah Winfrey

Greens

Greens evoke images of rockets, scientists, and Sherlock Holmes—all representing investigative and inquisitive minds. Greens are conceptual, seeking the big picture. They are independent thinkers at a sophisticated level. They enjoy designing and improving whatever they are working on. Their heads will rule over their hearts in making decisions. We depend on them to be calm, cool, and collected in the face of chaos.

They are attracted to careers in science and mathematics, engineering, information management, technology, strategic planning, and law. On the average, Greens, like Blues make up twelve to fifteen percent of the population, but the female-male proportions are reversed. Female Greens (thirty percent) make up three to five out of every one hundred people, and male Greens make up eight to ten of one hundred.

John Gray's description of a man-woman love relationship in *Men Are From Mars, Women Are From Venus* reflects a Blue Venutian and a Green Martian. Being goal-oriented and solution-oriented, "a man's sense of self is defined through his ability to achieve results" (p. 16). On the other hand, "a woman's sense of self is defined through her feelings and quality of her relationships" (p. 18) as she taps into her intuitive powers to assume the role of nurturer. Communications break down from speaking in different languages and symbols.

A Green husband, for example, gives a state-of-the-art calculator to his Blue wife for her birthday. Nice, expensive, one-of-a-kind gift. It doesn't thrill her. She would probably have liked instead an exotically scented designer candle on a delicately sculptured brass stand, or a dozen long-stemmed roses. Many of us buy gifts we ourselves want, rather than choosing one that the recipient would enjoy.

Greens become stressed in the following situations:

  Confusion arising from unclear goals and objectives

  Chaos, lack of control

No time to analyze and study and lack of options
Unfairness
Repetition and redundancy
Small talk
Emotional display

Greens are most cooperative when they are:
Dealing with discovery, asking questions
Being competent and intelligent
Developing a new approach and alternatives
Being recognized for their ideas
Given time to think
Gathering data, experimenting, testing hypotheses

Famous people perceived to be Greens are:
Maya Angelou
Albert Einstein
Mohandas Gandhi
Bill Gates
Martin Luther King, Jr.
Abraham Lincoln
Jacqueline Kennedy Onassis

In *King Warrior Magician Lover*, Robert Moore and Douglas Gillette discuss four personality types as the archetypes of mature masculinity (and femininity). They are symbolized by the King, Warrior, Magician, and Lover. By superimposing the *True Colors* metaphor on these images, each can be associated with a dominant color. The energetic, decisive Warrior casts an Orange hue, while the Magician, "the knower and master of technology" favors Green (p. 98). The Gold King has the ability to seek order, receive laws, and pass them on to others, and the sensitive and vivid Blue Lover reaches out to others and keeps the other three personalities humane. The application of *True Colors* to other metaphors helps us expand our knowledge of people.

Whether or not a color represents the majority or minority of the population does not seem to make any difference in that color's contribution and impact on civilization. Blues and Greens, along with the majority Oranges and Golds, have worked to make the world a better place. Our heroes and heroines represent all colors.

Since we have within us all four colors, we should have as a goal to build and draw from the strengths of each color to rejuvenate ourselves and others. The interplay of the primary and secondary colors often balances the strong characteristics of each color, resulting in a blend of colors. And the more blended our colors are, the more balanced we become.

Application of the True Colors Metaphor

The applications of *True Colors* for families and classrooms are limitless. The *True Colors* concept provides common language and tools for improving relationships between family members and in accentuating parental skills. *True Colors* provides focus and purpose, and generally a better understanding of ourselves and each other. We begin to appreciate commonalities among people, as well as their uniqueness and talents. Our awareness of ourselves and of others heightens communication skills, and we begin to view teaching/learning creatively.

True Colors improves classroom interactions not only between teachers and students, but also between students and students. Because *True Colors* is user-friendly, students can readily *guesstimate* the color of their teacher, their classroom and their school. And their estimation will likely be accurate.

A veteran teacher, with an excellent reputation in the classroom, felt like a novice last year. Of the five classes she taught each day, her last class completely drained her energy and humor. She described the climate as an emotional battleground, and she felt like walking away, which, of course, she would never have done. She dreaded going to this class, which was made up of seniors and a few juniors. Then, she and her class went through the *True Colors* process for one week, and the change in the classroom climate was remarkable. The teacher was solid Gold with a second Blue. The primary color of two-thirds of this class was bright Orange with Gold as its very last color. In fact, there were no primary Golds in the class, hence, no balance in its spectrum of colors. The teacher and students began to have conversations about past patterns of interactions that were aimed at irritating each other. Defining the environment in the *True Colors* context made all the difference. It was one of those "ah-ha" moments and ended up on a happy note. By adapting her teaching style, relationships and academic performance improved. The students worked consciously to build their Gold traits. The teacher's other four classes were a balanced mixture of Blues, Golds, Oranges, and a few Greens. *True Colors* deepened relationships that were working well.

True Colors need not be an addition to an already crowded curriculum. It is a tool for a teacher to deliver lessons more effectively. Creating and designing curriculum, its delivery, strategy, and method of assessment based on *True Colors*, could encourage students to learn more efficiently.

Using Social Studies and Language Arts as examples, *True Colors* helps sharpen students' ability to:
- compare and contrast (in Colors).
- interpret facts and behaviors, past and present (in Colors).
- problem solve (representation and cooperation of all Colors).
- analyze and synthesize (incorporating processes of all Colors).

For example, by studying a presidential election, students should be able to:
- analyze the candidates by Colors.
- explain and defend their choice of elected official.
- analyze their rationale, Color the major issues.
- discuss specific needs of a region and nation by Colors.

In another example, a teacher infused *True Colors* into the unit being taught on Richard Wright's *Black Boy* and the theme of the 1920s Harlem Renaissance. The teacher had students analyze the *True Colors* spectrum of each character and asked them to give reasons for their choices. In addition, students analyzed the conflicts in the novel, as well as the tone and mood created by the author. In these activities, students stepped up to a higher level of thinking.

Meeting standards are on the minds of educators today. Students from across the nation are being tested according to national and state standards for academic performance. In Washington State, curriculum is being aligned with Essential Academic Learning Requirements (EALRs). As an example, the lessons mentioned above correspond with the following EALRs.

Social Studies

—1.3 History: Examine the influence of culture on the
U.S. Interpret culture through colors.

—3.2 History: Analyze how historical conditions
shaped the emergence of ideas and how ideas changed
over time.

—3.3 Geography: Examine cultural characteristics,
transmission, diffusion, and interaction.

—1.2 Civics: Examine the key ideals of U.S. democracy
(respect for individuality and indivisibility of a nation).

—4.1 Civics: On individual rights; discussion of rights
and individuality.

Discussion on the rainbow concept of the United States and immigration.

Reading

—1.4 Understand elements of literature—fiction.

—2.1 Comprehend important ideas and details.

—2.2 Expand comprehension by analyzing, interpreting, and synthesizing information and ideas.

—2.3 Think critically and analyze an author's use of language, style, purpose, and perspective.

—3.3 Read for literary experience.

Writing

—1.1 Develop concept and design.

—1.3 Apply writing conventions.

—3.1, 3.2, 3.3, 3.4 Prewrite, draft, revise, edit.

These are only samplings of how one could align standards to lessons and *True Colors*. The implications are limited only by one's imagination. The following is a sample lesson in analyzing the media.

SAMPLE LESSON
True Colors and the Media
Ann Kashiwa & Lorinda Richer

General Objective: Students will be able to apply the concepts
                       of *True Colors* in analyzing the media.

For: Grades 6-12
Recomm. time frame: Minimum of three class periods,
                       four may be better
                       1. Introduction of *True Colors* and
                          identifying one's colors, and discussion
                          of *True Colors* and their characteristics.
                       2. Application to the media.
                       3. Assessment.

Specific Objectives:

1. **Know and understand the *True Colors* metaphor**

   Understand the concepts of *True Colors*.

   Identify one's primary, secondary, third and fourth colors.

   Discuss the strengths, joys, values, needs, and stresses of each
      color and their relevance to the class.

   Analyze learning and teaching styles.

2. **Apply the *True Colors* metaphor to mass media**

   View one of the following programs and focus on its sponsors
      (TV commercials).

News	Specials
PBS	Movie
Sitcom	Children's, including cartoons

3. **Complete the worksheet, which will help in analyzing the
   advertisements.**

Assessment:

1. Give a brief oral presentation to the class on the research you have completed.

2. Choose one ad that you would change to appeal to your primary and secondary colors.

3. By grouping in their faintest colors (4th colors), students will write or perform an ad that would appeal to this color.

4. Extra credit: Find examples of ads that represent each color and give an oral and/or visual report that analyzes the purpose of the ads.

This lesson meets the following EALRs (Essential Academic Learning Requirements established by the state of Washington):

Writing: 2. The student writes in a variety of forms for different audiences and purposes. Communication: 1. The student uses listening and observation skills to gain understanding. 2. The student communicates ideas clearly and effectively. 4. The student analyzes and evaluates the effectiveness of formal and informal communication, particularly in analyze mass communication.

SAMPLE LESSON
Worksheet #1 • *True Colors* and the Media

Name:_____

My True Colors are: (1) _____ (primary)

(2) _____

(3) _____

(4) _____ (least)

Name of the T.V. program:_____

Type of program:_____

Channel:_____

The T.V. commercials item(s) being sold	Primarily appeals to which color(s)	How? List ways Your perception

Choose one advertisement and tell how you would make it more appealing to your primary and secondary colors: _____

_____

_____

_____

Chapter 6

CHILDREN AT THE MILLENNIUM

No Time for Dawdling

Fifty years can seem like two hundred years when we consider the dramatic changes in lifestyles and national priorities over the last half-century. The post World War II era, in which I grew up, painted clear pictures of right and wrong, family and community, being American, education, and success. We had a definition of progress. At the dawn of the millennium, the painting is no longer as clear, as we deal with individuality and choice, concept of family, redefining the balance between ecology and human needs, advances in technology, children's issues, and what schools should be. There are many opinions about key issues and how to solve them.

Time is running out for schools. A sense of urgency permeates current thinking. Twenty years ago, Alvin Toffler in *The Third Wave* predicted civilization's demise if we fail to adapt quickly to the Third Wave (Information Age) from the Second Wave (Industrial) and First (Agricultural). The first two waves depended on a few educated people, while the Information Age relies on a large educated work force. This fact is arguable at a time when the dropout and illiteracy rates are alarmingly high in the United States.

There is no time for complacency. Ernest Boyer, President of the Carnegie Foundation for the Advancement of Learning, cautioned the educational community in 1983. Confusion over curriculum, parental involvement, character education, ethics, and morals need to be defined and clarified without delay. We need a shared vision wherein communities build relationships and a culture.

Many of us as educators view high school as the *Last Chance Place* for students who are struggling to become adults. Here, teachers should stop and give them the time of day. Here, students should be able to find at least one adult who cares. Here, many eyes should be focused on them—teachers and support staff, community liaisons, parents, peers, and supervisors at job sites. The three-strikes-and-you're-out philosophy should not be adhered to here, and students should be given many chances for success. Ours should be a more forgiving culture, while at the same time reaching for high standards in academic performance and behavior.

Students, who by their own admission goofed off during their younger years, begin to take themselves more seriously in high school. If we can keep them from giving up, we will begin to see a turnaround during their 11th grade year. The largest number of dropouts occurs at the end of their 10th grade year or at the beginning of their 11th grade year. This is usually preceded by two abysmal years. The odds for failing grades, inadequate credits, truancy, and discipline problems are overwhelming for a sixteen-year-old. They can easily give up.

These issues are of crisis proportions. They needed to be fixed yesterday. Societal problems spill—no, gush—into classrooms. The statistics are appalling: Sixty-five percent of children who live in poverty are between one and five years old. Other issues cloud the educational process of youngsters:

Wide gaps in socio-economic levels

High dropout rates among teenagers

High unemployment

Homelessness

Domestic instability

Mental and physical health issues

Addictions to drugs and alcohol

Violence

The November 29, 1999 *Seattle Times* reinforces the crisis. An article listed the top five threats to children as "teen pregnancy, abuse and neglect at home, inadequate child care, poor schools and lack of health care…"

Teachers don't deal with statistics; they deal with people. They accept children as they are and work forward from that point. If teachers could, they would cordon off students to keep them safe long enough to teach them life skills.

Our ideal finished product—a healthy individual—would stand shoulder-to-shoulder with a worldwide work force, problem solve creatively in a hi-tech global environment, seek the commonalities among people, and collaborate with a diverse population. Today, we have the most challenging situation schools have ever faced.

A flyer circulated in the faculty room drives home this point. "We expect our teachers to handle teenage pregnancy, substance abuse, and the failings of the family. Then we expect them to educate our children." John Sculley, Chairman and CEO of Apple Computers, wrote this in 1990 in urging public-private partnerships.

The challenge is to have all students reach higher standards and to close the achievement gap between non-achieving and achieving schools. One of the many organizations focused on improving education is the Institute for K-12 Leadership, which is partnered with the University of Washington and WestEd, a nonprofit education agency. Many other private corporations have adopted schools—for instance, QFC and McCaw—and large donors, such as the Gates Foundation for Education, help level the playing field so all children might have an opportunity.

We have a legal and moral obligation to meet this challenge. This charge has become increasingly difficult to fulfill, however, in a highly complex, post-industrial society governed by different criteria suggesting what kids should know.

Grassroots Reforms

This urgency has propelled school reforms in each state. Although reforms are unique, there are similarities. Furthermore, the phenomenon of school reform is worldwide. As the world *shrinks*, our achievements and problems become theirs and theirs become ours.

Through grassroots efforts, each school district has customized its reforms according to student and community strengths and needs. District curriculum is coordinated along state guidelines, such as the Washington State Essential Academic Learning Requirements (EALRs), approved by the State Legislature in February 1997. Pilot testing was done in 1998 at grade intervals (4th, 7th and 10th). Mastery in eight areas of study is (and will be) assessed—Reading, Writing, Communication, Mathematics, Science, Social Studies, Arts and Health/Fitness. The most noticeable difference between the past and present testing is the emphasis on higher-level thinking skills in all eight categories, and the students' ability to communicate.

The current push for restructuring is rooted in ideas seeded a generation ago. One of the predecessors to many of the current restructuring models was the Model School Project at Mariner High School in Everett, Washington. One-third of the students were on the free or reduced lunch program. Dropout rates were high. This rural-suburban community was home to a large number of transient families. As the first high school in the Mukilteo School District, Mariner opened its doors in 1970 with a dream of nurturing and challenging young people and keeping them in school.

1970s	*1990s*
Mariner Concepts	*Current Practices at Various Schools*
A caring school	Positive school climate; lower dropout rates
Student centered	Student makes decisions about learning
Advisor-Advisee program	Advisory and mentorship programs
Critical learning path	District and state requirements (EALRs)
Extended learning	Electives, extended day programs, work study
Learning styles	Multiple intelligences, emotional intelligences
Collaboration	Cooperative learning; learning teams
Interdisciplinary	Core curriculum
Team teaching	Grade and across-grade-level teams, pods
Community liaison	Social services; adopt-a-school programs
Non-graded report cards	Rubrics, multiple assessment
Individualized progress	Outcome/performance based
Flexible scheduling (A,B, and AB days)	Block; four-period day Year-round school

THE MARINER MODEL, 1972*

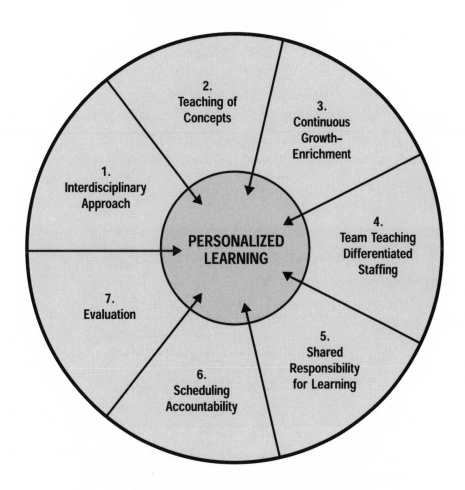

*Kathy Boardman and Ann Kashiwa, "Individualized Learning in Practice,"
Steps Toward Greater Individualizing for Small Schools,
Report of a Summer Institute, Oregon Small Schools Program, 1972.

THE MARINER MODEL, 1972
Summary of the Concepts

1. **Interdisciplinary Approach**

Integration of knowledge and skills.

Three divisions: Humanities, Practical Vocational/
Physical Education, and Math/Science.

Curriculum centered around themes, i.e., "The American
Dream" and "Man's search for Utopia" for 11th and
10th grades Language Arts and Social Studies,
respectively.

2. **Concept Approach**

Concept approach as opposed to subject approach.

Varied approaches and activities to reach the objectives.

3. **Continuous Progress**

Level system whereby students progress at their own
speed.

Lid taken off top; students may exceed required credits.

Critical pathways (sequenced; essential to the course, all
must learn).

Horizontal enrichment (moves on to another course).

Vertical enrichment (pursues in-depth, specialized work).

Two fifteen-week terms and one six-week term called
Mini-term.

Mini-term enabled students to complete courses
not finished in 30 weeks; courses were re-taught.

Six-week opportunities for *Exploratory* (white water
rafting, ice skating, cake decorating, cartooning) and

> *In-depth* "Reading for Pleasure" *(Anna Karenina, Hawaii),* pottery, rocket design and building.

4. Interdisciplinary Team Teaching/Differential Staffing

Two Language Arts teachers, two Social Studies teachers, and two teacher's aides made up the Humanities teaching teams for grades 9, 10, and 11.

Teams shared common planning time and pods.

Fostered collegiality.

Ad hoc teams were formed according to specific needs of students, i.e., between Electronics and Humanities, or between Mathematics, Science, and Humanities.

5. Shared Responsibility for Learning

Student given freedom and responsibility for learning/earning credits.

Guided by sixty-forty ratio: sixty percent student talk and forty percent teacher talk.

Encouraged interactions between students.

Emphasis on large group presentations followed by small group discussions and individualized instructions.

6. Scheduling and Accountability

Performance outweighed attendance (seat time); Carnegie units flexed.

Flexibility to allow a student to pursue in-depth projects.

7. Evaluation

Level system: completion of ten levels equals one credit.

Minimum requirement for Humanities (Social Studies/Language Arts) in one year equals forty levels, or four credits

May earn enrichment credits for extra credits.

Absence of letter grades.

No failures. Students were re-taught until their work was
at an acceptable level of performance (comparable to a
"C." "D" and "F" were unacceptable. *Failure was not an
option.*

Depended on computer-generated comments or
personalized comments by teachers. Was never a
problem for college admission.

Rising SAT scores

In 1980, Cliff Gillies, former Mariner High School
Principal and Assistant Superintendent of the Mukilteo
School District, appeared before the U.S. House
Subcommittee on Elementary, Secondary, and
Vocational Education of the Committee on Education
and Labor. One of the issues was how and why SAT
scores of Mariner students improved over the years
while scores across the nation were declining. Mr.
Gillies did not have a definitive answer, but believed the
answer was in the Advisor-Advisee program.

The Advisor-Advisee Program

The theme, *Personalized Learning*, was centered in the
Advisor-Advisee program. Using the Western Washington
University's Kuder Interest Inventory, advisors (teachers,
administrators and support staff) were matched with a group of
fifteen to eighteen advisees (students, grades 9-12). As advocate, counselor, registrar, confidant, teacher and friend, the

advisor made personal connections with the students and their families throughout their four years of high school. If an advisee got into trouble, the advisor sat in the conference in the vice principal's office.

The groups met for twenty minutes twice a week, or more if warranted by an individual situation. Field trips by advisor-advisee groups were annual events. Intervention by an advisor was critical to a student's success. If there were poor communications between a teacher and a student, a teacher frequently sought the help of the student's advisor, who acted as a troubleshooter. Communication between teacher and student almost always improved. An advisor could talk to a student in a way that a teacher could not. In many instances, the bonds have continued for nearly thirty years. The bonding was not only between adult and student, but also between adult and adult. These bonds have lasted through the second generation of Mariner graduates.

Over a twenty-year period, the Mariner Model School project has evolved into a more traditional high school. As far as I know, there was never a longitudinal study on the Mariner's experience. From my perspective, however, there were many factors that contributed to its changes, although it continued to hold on to some of its earlier concepts. Lack of funding was a major factor. Continuous restaffing and connection with the old-timers were difficult to fund as we were experiencing a budget crunch. One of the changes was in curriculum. Many of the special needs students were included into regular classes. A Learning Support Center (LSC) was created to give students extra tutoring during the school day, as well as before and after school. The LSC was manned by a certificated teacher and at least four teacher's assistants in the Humanities, Mathematics, Sciences, and Health. Advanced Placement and college preparatory courses were added for those wishing to pursue a more rigorous academic challenge.

As the school population increased, and, as more and more teachers were hired, departments replaced divisions, advisee-advisor contacts were decreased, and letter grades were instituted. The most challenging task of "Personalized Learning" was based on the daily monitoring of student progress without the use of computers. Our inability to keep track of students, whose progress was checkered all across the board, caused frustrations. Lack of support staff and increased class sizes added to the difficulty of personalizing education. Today, however, the staffs at Mariner and Kamiak, the school district's newest high school, continue to value the tradition of doing "what is best for kids."

Building Competence and Confidence

As in preceding centuries, philosophical, scientific, and technological advances have significantly changed today's patterns of society. Technology has literally shrunk the world, not only in terms of geography and distance, but also in how we make our livings. In the Puget Sound region, for instance, ten out of one hundred jobs are related to international trade, a $110 billion industry. The ratio will likely increase dramatically during the present decade. Therefore, our students will have to be trained in establishing relationships with culturally diverse populations locally and globally. They will need to behave as both citizens of their community and of the world.

Technology has also changed our communication patterns by revolutionizing the way we process information. The capabilities of the computer seem limitless, and yet we must train our students to function successfully in a world that we have yet to experience. Terms like Internet, Wednet, interactive learning, virtual reality, dot.com, and e-commerce are everyday language in our communication superhighway. The rapid rate of technical obsolescence keeps pushing us forward to learn and to adapt quickly. We spin faster and faster. Our high schools will have to meet this challenge if we want our graduates to be competent and competitive.

The makeup of our society has also changed. Former Washington State Superintendent Judith Billings quoted some revealing statistics for the last decade of the 20th century. The school population has increased sixty-five percent over the general population. Children, ages one to five, make up the highest group living in poverty. The number of children of color in our schools has surpassed previous projections. Given these facts, we need to address the issues of multiple languages and cultural diversity now. We need to understand the acculturation and assimilation process so that the American Dream does, indeed, offer hope to ALL our children. Teachers play a direct role.

The complexity of our society is furthermore demonstrated in the relationships of families and communities. Close and extended familial ties have been significantly altered, and in many instances severed. The need for closeness and intimacy is a major issue among the youth. If they do not find these at home or school, they will find them elsewhere, most likely in subcultures such as gangs. In fact, we are dealing today with a restless, angry population who are alienated from the mainstream.

Our institutions will have to re-create a sense of family and belonging in terms of structure, curriculum, activities, and atmosphere. Children without hope experience failure, separation, and alienation. The effects are devastating to the individual and to society.

Vision of a 21st Century School

In browsing through any bookstore, it is heartening to see many books about education and school reform. The topic is also highlighted in federal and state agendas. Commitments by former President Bill Clinton, his predecessors, and Washington State Governor Gary Locke about smaller class sizes, teacher preparation, professional development, safety, and community involvement have sparked more interest in educating our children. Many major businesses in Washington State, for example, are already committed to educational reforms, and have committed their dollars and services. With so much dialogue on reform, the first half of the 21st century could likely be the best education decades and could finally fulfill the dreams of early reformers.

The 1990 reformers shared a vision that called for systemic change and a new attitude about ourselves, each other, and our institutions. Sheryl Gunnel-Perry's *What in the World is Going*

On? (1998) elaborates on the Goals 2000 of the Bush adminis-tration (1989-1992) and the Department of Labor's "Secretary's Commission on Achieving Necessary Skills" report (SCANS). The Educate America Act, which established Goals 2000, and the SCANS report draw attention to raising academic standards and measuring competence in mathematics, English, science, foreign language, civics and government, economics, arts, his-tory and geography.

The SCANS report asked whether or not our children would have the skills, knowledge, and attitude to relate to a global marketplace. They would need to reflect upon and understand the complex issues of a new century. The questions asked were direct and to the point:

What are you learning/teaching?

Why are you learning/teaching it?

How will you use it?

Goals 2000 and SCANS were incorporated, elaborated, and infused into reforms across the nation. The National Association of Secondary School Principals (NASSP) addresses the "democratic imperative" to educate all children, because democracy and education are bound together in the tra-dition of the United States.

> "Education in a free society is a fundamental right and requirement for all—a cornerstone of American democracy. An educated populace is imperative." (p. 107)

The NASSP implores educators to break ranks, to rise above complacency and mediocrity, and to inspire and become "defender(s) of academic integrity" (p. 100). NASSP offers recommendations in all areas of high school education—curriculum, instruction, assessment and accountability, technology, organization and time, professional development, resources, governance, and ties to higher education and community.

Having considered the current and past research on educational reforms, I have concluded that for any systems change, to be effective in the 21st century, it must include all or parts of the following components.

A Caring School: A Home Away from Home

—Having an adult advocate.

—Building esprit de corps.

—Building esteem.

—Engaged in learning.

—Know "who I am" (via the *Dot, True Colors*).

—Co-curricular activities for a multitude of interests.

—Becoming an expert at something.

—Being special.

—Being in a safe physical and emotional environment.

Performance-Based Outcomes to Measure Student Learning

—Empowering students to make choices about what and how they will learn; personal plan for progress.

—Student accountability.

—High level of competence in academic, technological,
  and vocational training.
—Technologically astute population.
—Interdisciplinary/cross-disciplinary curriculum,
  including community and environmental resources.
—High level of thinking skills.
—Community service.
—Restructuring the schedule with flexible seat time.
—Year-round school.
—Create smaller structures: school within a school,
  houses of learning.
—Waiver of traditional graduation requirements.
—Meeting district, state, and national standards.
—Tutoring and re-teaching for at-risk students.

The Team Process

—Dialogue, collaboration, and consensus.
—People want to feel confident and proud about a product
  they help create.
—Working with diversity.
—Problem-solving by teams of students, staff, and
  community.

Delivery and Implementation of Instruction

—Direct instruction.
—Team teaching.
—Cooperative learning.
—Tutoring by peer or adult.

—Computer technology.

—On-the-job training.

—Mentorships.

Multiple Assessment and Evaluation Procedures

—Standardized testing.

—School-normed testing.

—State and national standards.

—Portfolios.

—Exhibitions.

—Oral assessment.

—Self evaluations.

—Group evaluations.

—Essays.

—Audiovisuals.

—Computer generated.

—Practicing and role-playing.

—Multi-media projects.

Community Partnership Models

—Building management.

—Community resources.

—Outreach programs.

—Volunteerism.

Budget

—Prioritization, re-organization, and restructuring of
  system.

—Design creative ways to allocate funds.

—Fully funded educational goals.

—Competitive salaries for personnel.

—Working with state legislatures.

Staff Development

Staff development is imperative for improvement and
reform. It not only refines instruction, it also increases staff collegiality and morale. Staff development further enhances communication and relationships within the school building,
beyond the immediate environment, out to state and national
levels. It rekindles the spirit to excel. Peer mentoring of new
teachers insures that the system can attract and keep the brightest and most caring entrants.

During the first decade of the 20th century, this nation was
vying to become a major player in global politics and a first-rate
economic power. Labor shortages prompted flows of people
from Europe and Asia to work in our factories, mines, fields,
and railroads. My grandparents, parents, and other Japanese
immigrated to the Hawaiian Islands during this period to labor
in the sugar cane and pineapple fields. The emphasis of public
education, not quite for the masses yet, was to *Americanize*
children of immigrants and prepare them for the agrarian or
industrial workplace.

In the first decade of the 21st century, this nation stands alone as the remaining superpower, whose standard of living is envied by other nations. We take for granted our material comfort and wealth. An anonymous fact sheet, titled "If the world could be shrunk to 100 people" was circulated in faculty rooms. The statistics are noteworthy.

> Six people would possess fifty-nine percent of the entire world's wealth, and all six would be from the United States.

Instead of *Americanizing* our students as we did in 1900, we should be asking what it would be like to be a citizen of the world? Educators will need to prepare students to create choices and become skilled decision makers. Students will need to access information, because only a fraction can be learned in school. Accessibility to information is the critical factor in leveling the playing field of learning. Through computerized educational programs, a child in a remote region needs to be able to learn as much as a child in an urban center.

Our students will need to become excellent in the basics: communication, mathematics, social and physical sciences, and technology. They will need to solve problems, alone and with other people. They will need to understand and accept team participation. This means getting along with a diverse population. It comes down to making connections with one's environment in the broadest sense.

Thirty years ago the Model School project was built around the concept of "what's good for students." When we queried students about what they wanted most from their school, they consistently replied, "A meaningful relationship with an adult." An article in *The Seattle Times* (September 6, 1999) entitled "What do children want most? A caring adult" spelled out this timeless need of every child. "The first thing kids want is someone who feels connected to them in a real way, who cares about them as an individual or a person," says Ellen Galinsky, President of the Families and Work Institute in New York. The caring adult, in addition to parents, could be someone at day care, at school, or in the neighborhood. Children need this kind of connection. Human needs transcend chronological years.

Having a meaningful relationship is a basic need of kids trying to grow up. In order to carry on the conversations that lead to these relationships, we need to know whom we are dealing with. Who are these children we are teaching today?

Chapter 7

WHO ARE THEY?

Only 14% of our teenagers feel they are considered to be of value by their community;

Only 22% reported that adult role models were a part of their everyday lives;

Only 23% reported their parents were involved in their schooling;

Even fewer, 17%, reported having a caring school climate;

43% of Seattle youth and 53% of Bellevue [Washington] youth attested that they considered resolving their conflict in a nonviolent way.

Pamela Eakes

Mothers Against Violence in America

The Seattle Times, May 11, 1997

3.5 hours—adolescents spend time alone;

11 hours fewer time spent between parent(s) and child, compared to the 1960s;

8000 murders seen by a child in all media by the end of elementary school;

300% increase in teen suicide since the 1960s;

1000% increase in teen depression since the 1950s.

John Cloud
"What can the schools do?"
Time, May 3, 1999

Every day 100,000 children carry a gun to school;

Every day 40 children are killed or injured by guns on school grounds;

Every hour 900 teachers are threatened in the schools;

Every hour 40 teachers are assaulted.

Youth Violence in the Schools
Spokane County Health District, Washington
Fact Sheet, Spring, 1996

Alarming statistics. Even more alarming are the kids caught in between the numbers. Can we get to them in time? Will we be able to reach out to them before they disappear and add to the dropout statistics?

The barrage of violence against persons and property has changed the school climate and put safety as the number one concern of schools. If our attention is consumed by the safety issue, it will siphon our energies and resources and derail reform efforts for the new century.

School shootings—at Moses Lake, Washington; Paducah, Kentucky; Jonesboro, Arkansas; Springfield, Oregon; Columbine, Colorado; and Conyers, Georgia—punctuate the last decade of the millennium, not an honorable distinction. Although these tragedies caused unspeakable pain to the victims and their families, as well as to the perpetrators and their families, they are the exceptions rather than the rules. But because these tragedies received headline attention, many assumed that a majority of the students are out-of-control adolescents. If we were to look only at statistics on violence, we might also believe that all teens are prone to violence and mayhem. They, of course, are not.

The vast majority of students are doing well, keeping up their grades, staying involved in activities, holding part-time jobs, volunteering in their communities, and focusing on their futures in the work place, universities, or armed services. The actions of a few forever touched all of our lives, but mostly those who directly suffered from the tragedies. The shootings forced us to reflect. In each case, the question most asked was, "How could it have happened here?"

Kids Are Still Kids

As adults reminisce about their own teen years, they tend to assume that things are like they used to be. In many ways, times are similar. Growing years are still painful, but at the same time, teen years represent energy, freedom, a carefree attitude, and fun. Kids are still kids. The following adjectives and descriptions capture some common characteristics among teens.

Energetic. An adolescent is like a spinning ball, full of energy. The adrenalin flows through him continuously and causes him to take action. When one's body and mind are growing at a rapid pace, they need a stable environment, some stability for all the energy. But if the environment is too restrictive, the ball will spin out of control, and become rebellious to any authority figure. If the environment is too loose, the ball can spin aimlessly.

In either case, the individual rides the tangents (+) and (-) and fails to reach the next level of growth ($\pm$). He may not experience the *Dot* (•) for a long while. A parent's or teacher's role is to harness that energy and help the child set his course for the future.

> Voted by her classmates as the freshman Homecoming princess, Regina was enthusiastic about school. She participated in student government, promoted food drives for the hungry, organized car washes, volunteered to fill Thanksgiving baskets, and waited on tables on weekends, all the while pursuing a tough schedule centered around marketing, travel, and tourism. Named an "Outstanding Graduate of 1999" by *The Seattle Times*, she was one of the movers in transforming a grassy area next to her high school into a children-centered park. She, her classmates, and community members raised $700,000 for an outdoor basketball court, a roller hockey rink, a skateboard area, a playground for young children, picnic areas, and restrooms. She could be seen on the construction site wearing a hard hat, a privilege she had earned.

Ambivalent. Full of contradictions. On one hand, confident, cocky, know-it-all, and self-absorbed. On the other hand, insecure and worrying about what others think of him. He can be lonely, vulnerable, and moody. His need to be independent and to be his own person often butts up against the adult world. A teen can also be understanding and compassionate towards an underdog. Brigette, for example, accompanied her dad every Friday night to feed and house the homeless at a downtown shelter. Jason coached a neighborhood basketball team at a local gym for young children.

Teens test their limits. They are faddish, just like teens of past generations. They like the preppie look, the sag and bag, and the perennial T-shirt and jeans or shorts. Some dress all in black: black lipstick and jet black hair. Sometimes they like orange hair. Body piercing and tattoos are "in." Being different is okay. They seek their individuality, but they also want to be like everybody else. Fitting in and belonging drive their behavior.

Belonging. To belong is probably the most powerful motivation in teen behavior. The teen is a social being and needs to be accepted. To be part of a group, needed, valued, and respected are critical. They contribute to a teen's happiness or depression, and whether or not he likes school. He needs to feel special. He will seek it any way he can.

> Randall was small for his age. Diagnosed with ADHD (Attention Deficit Hyperactivity Disorder), he took Ritalin, which he would have skipped if he could. He was sociable

and loud. He continually hung around other students, and liked doing favors for them. Being accepted by the group was important to him. He ached to be special in and out of the classroom. Eventually, his way of being special got him into trouble with the law. He ran with a group whose illegal activities included stealing cars from the rental car lots. One day I saw Randall cruising with his buddies in a new van. He was only 15 and didn't have a license to drive.

Merrill was an extraordinarily bright and focused junior, who was a year younger than her peers for having skipped a grade. Her grades were outstanding, she was involved in band and academic quiz competitions, and she had the advantage of having a nurturing, affluent family. On the exterior, she was confident and buoyant but she says, in looking back at her teen years, "to belong" was her and her peers' concern. Being unsure, wanting to be needed, and feeling special were their common needs, though she and her peers were among the most adjusted and successful students.

Curious. Being curious and bold describe the teen years, too. Teen years are a time for discovering, experimenting, stretching, and testing the limits. Because of teens' perception that they are invincible, they boldly venture into risk-taking activities that test the limits of their man/womanhood. Teen years are also a period of sexual awareness, and teens begin to envision their future with a life-long partner. They think about long-term relationships.

Optimistic. This likely comes from teens' feeling of invincibility and the hope that their lives are going to be better than the lives of their parents and grandparents. Teens typically believe that things will work out, or they are convinced that no harm will come to them, even when they take risks.

Imaginative and creative. For those teens whose energies center around their creative spirits, producing beautiful products in the industrial and fine arts departments, composing music, writing fiction and poetry, and manipulating the computer to solve complex problems are common. They know how to have fun and to think up new games and challenges to test their minds and bodies.

Kids Can't Be Kids

While children are much the same yesterday and today, we teachers deal with a vastly different climate and clientele, unique to this decade. Many of us, who had been teaching children for three decades were blindsided by the emergence of a different population that was less receptive to traditional forms of teaching and learning, more vocal, more assertive, and more skeptical of authority.

There is irony in our lifestyle directions. Our way of life has become easier (i.e., less physical drudgery), and at the same time more complex (i.e., explosion of knowledge, changing relationships). One needs to be well educated and skilled to be productive and fulfilled. How do our children fare? I have observed the following characteristics that reflected the last two decades.

Affluent. Societal norms of having anything and everything at our fingertips became an accepted fact in America. The long period of peace and economic growth maximized our purchasing power. Quality goods in huge quantities and varieties are accessible to any citizen, who is often courted by slick ads to buy, buy, buy. The affluent lifestyle is apparent in all socio-economic levels—those who are rich, as well as those who barely subsist from day to day.

Take, for example, the annual event of the high school senior prom. The cost of the tickets, corsage and boutonniere, dinner at a fine restaurant, a limousine service, and late-night snack is between $375 and $600 per couple. These are 1997 estimates. An evening may cost up to $1,000 today. This does not include the cost of an evening dress or a rented tux, or the cost of a hotel room for the after-dance party, which is becoming a norm. Many work at their minimum wage jobs to save for this event.

This prom tradition is national and has extended to 9th graders "graduating" from junior high to senior high. They seek all the trimmings of a senior prom, including a chauffeur-driven limousine. As an alternative to after-prom parties at hotels, where temptations for drugs and alcohol exist, parents often host post-prom parties at their homes. This all-night vigil with snacks, pop, and fun activities keeps the partiers sober and off the streets.

Technological. Kids today are technologically savvy. They are comfortable with gadgets and computers. Technology has literally shrunk the world and opened it up to children. A 5th grade class in Seattle corresponds with 5th graders in Dublin or

Kyoto through the Internet. Now there is snail-mail or e-mail. The Internet has changed the ways children play games and do research. The information available on the Internet is mind-boggling. There can be danger in the information they receive and the persons with whom they are chatting. Children are still children and are naive about the ways of the world. They want to believe.

Stressed. Stress comes from growing up too fast, cantering out of control, feeling pressured by family, school, and work, eating poorly, and having no down time to think and reflect. Teens have no time to smell the roses. These are the common complaints by teens. Emotions and tempers are often heightened when demands on time are extreme.

According to teens, tensions in family relationships cause the greatest stress. Whether or not the family structure comprises original parents, single parent, or co-mingled families is not as critical as the relationships between the family members. Effects from divorces can linger on for five to ten years or longer; it takes that long to process the emotions.

Continued stress causes what I term "mental paralysis"— inability to concentrate and complete simple class assignments, and inability to get one's self up and moving.

Even though his parents pleaded with him and conferenced with teachers and administrators, Chris did not attend school regularly. He behaved as though he had completely given up on life. His parents thought he might be bi-polar. Nathan, on the other hand, came to school regularly, but sat like a log and refused to do any assignment. He didn't cause any disruption in class except in his failure to do school work. Both young men enrolled at an alternative school, but I suspect they later became dropouts.

Randi suffered from depression and stayed out of school half a year. According to her father, she could not get out of bed in the morning. When she came to school, she could not finish her day. A warm, attractive, intelligent young lady, Randi felt she had to be excellent and if she couldn't be excellent, why even try? She found school too stressful. After a second suicide attempt, her parents got her help at a mental health clinic. Leaning on her parents, psychiatrists, and counselors, she struggled through a period of healing. We were creative in designing her class schedule to help her during this difficult period of her life. She did better in her senior year. She did graduate and planned on going to college.

Teen choices of having to do everything and having to go everywhere are primary causes of stress. Teens cannot continue the pace of being a Super Teen without a heavy price.

Take Karin, a likely Orange-Green-Blue. Very smart and intense. Having been in the district's gifted program for many years, she enrolled in Advanced Placement and Honors classes in high school. Her extra-curricular activities centered around the arts and academics—drama, art, and quiz competitions. She also worked part-time. Her parents' divorce dislodged her "equilibrium," and she appeared disoriented as she began her senior year. One early morning, her father, with whom she was living, came looking for her, because she hadn't come home. She had run away. The rumor was that she had moved to a different city with an older boyfriend. I left word with her friends, who would not reveal her whereabouts, to have her call me collect, any hour. She called twice to say she was okay and promised to finish school, no matter what. I never learned the whole story of what precipitated this serious crisis. Seven years later,

I received an announcement of her marriage AND her impending graduation from a medical school in California.

Many students work twenty to thirty hours a week to purchase a car, pay for insurance (up to $1,000 per year for a male teen), and to buy brand name fashions, like $150 athletic shoes. Many of my students were so tired that they couldn't keep their eyes open or heads up in their morning classes. Some finished work at 11:00 p.m., which meant they went to bed about 1:00 a.m. and were up by 6:00 a.m. There are laws governing teen work hours, but they are not always enforced.

Stress levels among youths are incredibly high, especially if the youth is a serious student. Keeping up with grades, getting into the "right" college, playing sports, going to dances, maintaining a relationship, being part of a family, keeping a job—too many items on one's plate. Something usually gives, and it is often their health. Many are sleep-deprived and lose concentration.

We find capable students working below their potentials by opting for less challenging classes in order to maintain a high GPA. Habits of discipline and hard work are not always developed, and these poor habits catch up with them in college. Deadlines and grading criteria are more closely adhered to in college.

I urge students to cut back their work hours—way back—and be a dependent. I remind them that they will have the rest of their lives to work, whether they like it or not. They need to concentrate on their Number One job—to be a student. The money will surely follow.

Many teens are overwhelmed by their problems, which they think are not resolvable. They run away to live with friends, which can cause further stress. Temporary residences from one location to the next are not the answer. This actually causes more anxiety. Teens also enter into an adult relationship for the wrong reasons. Emotionally, most teens are not ready to cope with a serious relationship. Many drop out of school at this point. Some find full-time jobs, but many wander about. A number become homeless.

In every urban center, clusters of young, homeless boys and girls congregate. Many of them are runaways. Their "camp" attracts other youths in the area, which adds to the total population of the site. A former student, Michael Ko, wrote about the young homeless who reside in the Ravenna district, north of the University of Washington in Seattle. As a first-year reporter for *The Seattle Times*, he lived with the homeless for four days and nights in July 1998. He took with him his notebooks, a sleeping bag, ten dollars, and packs of cigarettes for bartering. To chronicle the homeless lifestyle, he wanted to understand. "They are bold world travelers, soul-searching hippies, brash runaways, abused adolescents, aimless wanderers. They are sane or deluded, drug savvy and life weary." More than anything else, they guard their independence.

If our children are so stressed out, shouldn't we be helping them debrief and de-stress? Prioritizing tasks and activities, accepting imperfections, and learning anxiety-reducing techniques (physical exercise, art, and play) would be a start.

Addicted. Cigarettes, drugs, and alcohol hook kids. School performance spirals downward for an addict. Attendance is first to go—tardiness, skipping classes or not showing up at all. Inability to concentrate and stay focused causes poor grades and threatens graduation goals. Erratic behavior leads to arguments, fights, assaults and other discipline problems for which a student can be suspended or expelled.

In order to sustain their addictive behavior, teens become sellers of drugs. Some become thieves to get money for what they need. Criminal offenses among the young have increased over the last two decades; many end up on probation or are incarcerated. Some are sent away for long periods to institutions, such as Greenhill and Echo Glen in Washington. If the addiction is not addressed—assessment, short- and long-term counseling, health care, support groups—the addict will surely drop out of school and have few skills to function in the adult world. They also suffer from poor nutrition and health.

> An only child and demonstrably loved by his mother, Kyle was a gentle, kind-hearted student with a friendly smile and wave. He was a cigarette smoker so he was always tardy to classes because he had to have one quick puff. He also smoked marijuana before and after school. In his junior year, he began to lose interest in school, his attendance was unpredictable, and his grades dropped. One day his mother called me, quite upset. He had withdrawn $300 with her ATM card. Kyle confessed to her that he had bought marijuana from a classmate, who had assured him that he could double that

amount in no time by breaking up the stash into small, sal-
able bags. The supplier of the marijuana was the seller's
father, according to his mother. She sent her son to a recovery center for a month. Teachers worked out his assignments
during this period. I hope he overcame his addiction and
graduated. He showed great promise.

Angry and violent. School staff members are predominantly
Golds and Blues. They like kids and want to help them grow up
to be good adults. But today's teens are more complex. Their
unpredictable, intense anger was something teachers were not
prepared to deal with. Coupled with the anger is the teens' fas-
cination with guns. In one unannounced locker check, we
found, pasted on the inside of a door, a photo of five female students, posed on a couch, carrying guns and sawed-off rifles.
This arsenal of weapons was in someone's home.

The following are some situations that concerned educators.

Heidi. During her freshman year, Heidi was a familiar
face in the assistant principal's office. She lost her temper
and fighting words came flying out of her mouth faster than
one could count to four. She argued, disrupted class with her
hostile attitude, and generally took a tough stance against
anyone who looked at her the wrong way. She was street
smart, independent, and an underachiever, but during those
rare moments, she would listen to advice about her abilities
and her future. She did respond to compliments. There were
more and more of those reflective moments during which she
was funny, charming, and honest. Things started to turn
around in her 10th grade year; her grades and attendance
improved, and her arguments were less frequent. She
returned to school in September as an optimistic junior. It
looked like she would indeed be the first one in her family to
graduate from high school.

Heidi, however, was extremely protective of her boyfriend. They argued daily. She did most of the screaming. In one of their heated arguments, she threw her lunch, a hot cup of noodles, in his face because he was "messing around with another girl." She didn't care that this happened in the middle of the commons with other students watching. Both she and her boyfriend were being treated for a sexually transmitted disease, and their relationship was rocky. Her grades dropped. Neither one of them completed their junior or senior years.

Kisha. Kisha was a vociferous, volatile, 5'3" 9th grade, who believed everyone was out to get her. In a confrontation, she would stand nose to nose with a 6'2" principal or a 6' security officer, all the time spewing out profanities. Because of her behavior, she was kicked out of every one of her classes. We tried to get help for her, but neither she nor her mother agreed to counseling. I suspect she was socially promoted throughout the years. She didn't remain in any one school long enough to be assessed and counseled. She was suspended for the remainder of the year for threatening staff members.

Travis. Slender, 5'6" Travis thought of himself as a cowboy from Montana. His black leather boots, felt hat, jeans, and bright blue pickup truck reinforced his image. He had a sense of humor about life and liked coming to school, though not necessarily to attend class. His language was liberally sprinkled with expletives. He was in the assistant principal's office often because of smoking and cutting classes. There were interesting conversations about places he'd lived and things he had done. He talked about his drinking binges, "only on weekends." His temper was not always evident, but when it flared up, he was uncontrollable. He once got into a fight off campus after school and overpowered the other student, kicking him brutally. One day, he sauntered onto campus, having missed his morning classes. He was intoxicated. When I spoke to his mother about this, she became angry with me for accusing her son. I told her that he drank more than "a bottle occasionally," and recommended drug and alcohol assessment and counseling before returning to school. She slammed the phone down. He dropped out of school.

Scott and Lin. They hardly knew each other, but there had been shared stares and words under their breaths as they passed each other in the halls. With friends on both sides egging them on, they came to blows during the passing time outside the building. By the time the security officer and staff got to the scene, the crowd circling the fighters was four-deep. The crowd was enjoying the fight. Lin's jaw was broken. Again and again, stares, words, and egos crossed the line between civility and violence.

The fact sheet from Spokane's Adolescent Health Education states: "Children and youth are ten times more likely to be victims of violence than to be arrested for violence." What strategies do we teach potential victims about victimization? The fact sheet reveals other statistics about violence and crime:

Every day in America, 5,702 children are arrested.

Every day 316 children are arrested for violent crimes.

There are 4,881 gangs in the U.S. with 249,324 members.

While gang activities have scaled down since the 1980s and gang task forces in the police departments have been abandoned, there are remnants still existing among those who survived the violent years. Certainly, the clothing (baggy, colors), music (rap), language (family, brotherhood, non-verbal signs, and signals), art (graffiti, tattoos), and mannerisms (stance, gait, dance) have become mainstream. By the mid-1990s, this subculture had become part of the dominant culture among adolescents.

In the 1980s, *T* was an ex-gang banger from Oakland. One brother was in jail, another was always in trouble, and he himself was deeply into the gang culture. His parents sent him north to live with his aunt so he could have a chance to succeed. He wore a dark, oversized parka with the hood over his head, and sat with his arms crossed, as if to say, "I dare you to teach me." He was a tough, sullen young man, big enough to play football on any defensive team. He couldn't play sports, though, because his grades were poor. He knew the ways of the street. Other students kept their distance at first. Underneath the cool exterior was a young man who was homesick, a little lonely, and wanting to succeed. We discussed what might have become of him had he returned to Oakland. "I'd be dead," he commented. So he stuck it out in Washington. He made friends, attended classes regularly, and earned credits. In his senior year, he was a very reliable Teacher's Assistant in one of my classes. He graduated and began a career in retail business. He has many talents.

Felix couldn't shake away from his gang family. He dropped out of school twice, but always returned with the renewed hope that he would finish high school. His discipline record was for truancy and nothing else. Sociable, funny, great big smile, sense of humor, clear, expressive eyes, he was supporting himself and living with various friends in the city. He said the gang members would never "let me go." In one of our many conversations, I asked him if he had family far away from Washington who would provide him an opportunity to start fresh without all the baggage. He didn't. He had relatives in California, but that was where he had started his gang affiliation. We agreed on an attendance contract and a modified schedule. He attended classes for four days and then he disappeared.

Weeper was his tag name. His parents were looking for him. So were the police. His parents came to school with their pastor, who was their interpreter. They looked distraught, exhausted, and frightened. I became choked up watching their struggle. They said he had run away a week ago, came home because he needed money, and promised to stick around until they got home from work. But when they had come home, he was gone, along with his clothes. They feared for his life because he was with "bad, bad boys." Tall and lean, he was gentle and shy in his demeanor. He was soft-spoken and polite. He did not reveal anything about what he was feeling or about his friends. I never got to know who he was or why he felt he had to be on the run.

Many children feel there is no point in going on. Unhealthy teens are a national concern. The February 8, 2000 headline in *The Seattle Times* shouts out, "Why are so many teens killing themselves?" In certain areas the rate of suicide increased by one hundred percent from 1980 to 1996. This tragedy affects everyone. Compulsive behavior, aggression, anger, violence impact the classroom. Control and discipline become problems. Good teaching is near impossible, or comes at a high cost to the teacher's energy and focus.

The innocence of the growing years is becoming a myth. The world has changed so much. Our young people deal with the serious, real-life issues of survival and self-esteem. Their life experiences transcend their chronological years, but their hearts and spirits are still sixteen. Their coping skills are unsophisticated and crude. We haven't adequately taught them these skills.

We are learning to diffuse their anger and channel it in less destructive avenues. Most importantly, we would like to teach students to become more resilient and to rechannel their energies elsewhere and more productively. We need to develop a whole array of strategies: counseling, adult and peer mentoring, conflict resolution, and *True Colors*, to name a few.

Even in the worst scenario, some kids remain resilient. They have these traits in common: "social competence, problem-solving skills, autonomy, and a sense of purpose and future." The most effective teachers understand the protective and caring factors of "high expectations, purposeful support, and participation" (Krovetz, *Fostering Resiliency*, pp. 64, 80). Teachers can intervene to make a real difference in a child's life. Teaching can become an art in creating the kind of atmosphere that allows students to get in touch with their *Dots*.

Chapter 8

A TEACHER: BEING AN ARTIST

Attitude of an Artist—Brushing the Dot

Any person who is involved in directing the growth and maturity of a student is a teacher. Most people assume that "a teacher" is a certificated staff member at a school. In a broader sense, a teacher is also an educational paraprofessional, principal, counselor, coach, bus driver, janitor, cook, parent, and many others.

I find it impossible to separate the two phenomena of learning and teaching. The processes overlap. Doing them well is an art. Artists interpret human experience and communicate perspectives that are unique. Artists are individuals whose intellects, emotions, and imaginations enable them to view the dichotomies of life and to synthesize that which is basic (*Dot*).

Artists share common qualities. They are highly disciplined, committed, and persistent in searching for truth. They are bold in extending beyond themselves and beyond the norms of society. They attempt to communicate an element of truth that applies to universal humanity. They are passionate about what they do. They free themselves from bias and prejudice. To artists, politics, religion, race, sex, and socio-economic strata are artificial barriers that tend to impede the communication of truth. Boundaries, which separate nations and individuals, become irrelevant.

Through their selection process, artists transform disorder to order. They may not overtly change anything "out there," but they may change our *perception* of "out there." They mentally package and organize hundreds of facts and priorities. They create a new vision of their world, and their contribution to civilization is their expression of this vision.

Vehicles that lead us to a truth are many: writing, singing, painting, running across a football field, balancing on a beam, or doing something hardly noticeable. An artist can be anyone: a neighbor who is a master carpenter, a gourmet cook, an academically handicapped child who is learning to add and subtract for the first time. An artist turns failure into success by welcoming all experiences and trying again and again. An artist inspires us to stretch.

At the close of the millennium, there was no shortage of disharmony, discontent, insecurity, and mental and physical illness. It can appear that artistry has been forgotten, but we still gravitate to that which is beautiful and harmonious. We still love the mastery of skills in academics, athletics, and interpersonal relationships. In a complex world, there is yet a need for artists who can simplify the complex. The artistic process begins with the artist-teacher, who in turn teaches students to be artists.

How do schools nurture artists? If we could graphically illustrate learning, we would probably see the nurturing taking place on several planes, with each pupil on different levels and different locations on a plane. Picture a three-dimensional cube symbolizing the (+) (-) (±). How can we make sense of this complexity?

First, provide opportunities to master all aspects of human endeavors to balance physical and mental development. There already exists a structure through physical education, humanities, languages, science, math, and technology. They all fall under the umbrella of the arts. By the end of his 12th year, a student's record should be a representative of human experiences.

To be an artist demands expertise in knowledge and skills. It requires a high level of achievement and should be the primary objective of curriculum. A student needs to be challenged to seek and should see himself as progressing, improving, and gaining confidence and assurance.

Raising the bar. In the early 1980s education moved toward raising the standards among high school populations. The district board of directors adopted the policy of schoolwide testing, much like final exams in college. In addition, several of us teachers piloted courses in the IB (International Baccalaureate), as well as in the AP (Advanced Placement) programs. Under the support and leadership of Principal Dr. Suzanne Simonson, our school chose to focus on the AP programs, which included subjects in U.S. History, Modern European History, English Language, Literature, Calculus, and French. Eventually, the AP program expanded to the subjects of Chemistry, Physics, Government, and Art.

Students and parents were pleased with the AP test results, which meant savings in tuition at college, and, even more important, students were prepared to meet the academic challenges of a university.

Initially, we who taught the AP and IB courses struggled to reach a higher level of skill, knowledge, attitude, and thinking. We AP teachers felt the pressure of accountability as we prepared our students for the exams. Most of our students rose to our expectations. Contrary to the students' opinion regarding hard work, there were no long-term adverse reactions from "putting out one hundred percent," or from losing sleep occasionally.

The bar was also raised for those not enrolled in the AP classes. Higher-level thinking activities were encouraged for the entire student population. Frequently, identical assignments were given to AP and non-AP students, with the major difference in the length of time each group spent on assignments.

The *Dot* is an expression of an artist's balance and the integration of his *True Colors*—Orange, Gold, Blue and Green. When a person operates from his *Dot*, his color spectrum is balanced, drawing upon the specific strengths of each of his colors. His mental and physical energies are aligned with his environment. He experiences the "oneness," which philosophers describe as the moment of perfection and awareness. If one could visualize his *True Colors* spectrum, the strengths in each of his colors would appear synchronized to perform a single act, whether in sports, drama, writing, or other activities.

True Colors is also a metaphor for a school. GREEN (cerebral) represents the goal of creating thinkers and skillful artisans. ORANGE (kinesthetic) represents the application of ideas by doing. BLUE (heart) reflects the relationships between people. GOLD (physical) creates the environment necessary for students to learn and succeed. When a student recognizes his *Dot*, learning becomes relevant and he is motivated to become better.

A true artist needs self-discipline, despite the popular misconception of an artist being free-spirited.

An artist needs clearly defined guidelines for conduct. He needs to be committed to attendance, to try, to be curious, and to be kind.

The "Bubble Up and Trickle Down" theories, relating to government and economics, can also be applied to human development. In an environment where students interact on high academic and emotional levels, benefits "bubble up." In such an atmosphere, another Michelangelo might emerge as the genius. The inspiration of brilliant individuals will inevitably affect others who are trying. Their genius trickles downward to benefit all.

Artistry in athletic endeavors is very visible. We encourage young people to participate in order to develop themselves physically and mentally. The skills, discipline, and dedication of an athlete can be miraculously transferred to his work in the classroom, his academic achievements and interpersonal relationships. On the other hand, winning has too often become all-important so that the reason for developing a balanced person is lost. John Devine and Cliff Gillies bring this point home to coaches and parents in *Victory Beyond the Scoreboard.*

America needs a fresh look at sports. The Vince Lombardi approach, "Winning isn't everything—it's the only thing" does not have a place in youth sports. Only the top three percent of young athletes will become consistent winners and athletic stars. The "win-at-all-costs" philosophy neglects the other ninety-seven percent, and in fact, doesn't teach the right values to the winners either.

Learning lifelong values—values which are the behavioral foundation of honest workers, sensitive leaders, strong families, civic-minded neighbors, and capable parents—is the quintessential benefit of sports (p. 1).

A runner must practice miles and miles in both the cold and in the heat before he becomes a superb marathoner. A wrestler must exercise his muscles and stamina to achieve excellence. A cartoonist must draw thousands of faces before his hands move smoothly across the page. For only a glimmer of perfection in any field, many hours of practice are required.

Many people stop short of mastering an activity, because it demands too much effort. Their psychological and physical threshold for pain would be low without a stick-to-it attitude and a vision of where they are going. However, this can be changed.

A teacher is the conduit between the learner and what he is being learned by tailoring the content to the learner. A teacher should recognize the artist in each pupil, and should communicate the ultimate goal. A teacher should inspire a pupil to pursue and refine mastery of his talent. The teacher should be an opportunist who creates windows of opportunity to open teachable moments.

"Let me hear about you someday—that you have broken a world record in high jump, or have found a new cure for a human ailment, or saved someone's life, or have a painting hanging at the Seattle Art Museum, or have been a family person with happy, healthy children…"

This was my hope to the graduating seniors to explore and touch their potential and to keep in touch.

An artist is like a rose: his beauty is not in analysis, but in himself. We, in a free society, place value not only on the end result, but in the process. Teaching dwells in the process. We should help students to understand who they are and to choose what they will become.

SOME TIPS ON "HOW TO" FROM A THIRTY-YEAR VETERAN, WHO CONTINUES TO BE A STUDENT

Asking the Right Questions

What are they learning?

Why are they learning it?

How will they use it?

Envisioning a Goal

It begins with articulating a goal for the course, such as 11th grade U.S. History, a required course for graduation. Start with a big picture of what U.S. History should be to students. What should be the end result, and what will the process be? Is there a theme, a thread that runs throughout the year? For example, "Individual freedom and social responsibility: Improving self and society in search of the American Dream." Historically, there has always been tension between individual freedom and group security, and each generation has attempted to balance the two. How is this tension being resolved today?

Identifying what is Important about my Course

Identify six to twelve basic concepts and skills that every student should learn. The Critical Path, a concept developed by the Mariner High School staff in the 1970s, identified the "have-tos" of each course. Every student had to master a designated number of concepts and skills, determined by the team of teachers teaching the course. Superimposed and running parallel to the Critical Path were the Enrichment Units. One type of Enrichment Unit was to have students explore related concepts on an introductory level. We called this "horizontal exploration." The other type, called "vertical exploration," allowed students to study a single topic in depth after they had mastered the critical concepts and skills.

Teaching to Scholarly Pursuit of Content and Promoting Higher-level Thinking Skills

Study, understand, and practice Bloom's taxonomy, Piaget's thinking order, Gardner's seven intelligences, and all the major contributors to educational theories and practices. And what traits will students with a scholarly attitude have? They will be curious and interested; they will know a lot, having a broad base of knowledge; they will work hard and they will solve problems through their language of respect.

Teaching students to think and write was my goal. I critiqued their every sentence, every idea, and communicated with them through copious annotations and one-on-one conferences. After a month or two, they saw how much they had changed and that in itself became a motivator to learn. Writing seems to improve plateau by plateau, so discouragement arises when students feel that they have stopped improving. Frequently, improvement comes in such small increments that the learner feels he is not moving at all. The teacher needs to be a cheerleader on the sideline.

Writing helps a student grow as a scholar and as a person. Because many students dislike writing, they have to be convinced that there is a higher goal in learning to analyze and synthesize. Writing is a way to better understand themselves. My writing assignments were directed toward encouraging substance and depth to enable students to understand historical perspective and how they fit into history. In teaching them to think and write, I looked for their developing a strong hypothesis, a logical sequence of events and thoughts, persuasive evidence to prove their thesis, and their ability to critically analyze and tell a story. History is, after all, the story of human events.

Grabbing their Interest and Imagination

Choose projects and units that relate/connect to the lives of your students. Create a sense of passion in seeking a solution to a problem. Projects have to be challenging and doable at the same time. Set parameters to help them focus—if the question is too broad, the response will tend to be broad and shallow. Work toward complexity and depth, appropriate to the level of your students. Appropriate use of analogies and metaphors will enhance the "ah-ha" moments, create mystery, and peak students' curiosity. Vary activities, keep them guessing and looking for more. Recognize that you are teaching to a diverse student population. Make sure all their *True Colors* are addressed.

An imaginative and skillful teacher can hook students in reading almost anything, including Shakespeare's *Hamlet*. I once observed Ms. Celia Koehler as she was leading a discussion on Hamlet's relationship with his mother and stepfather. Her students were 10th and 11th grade Special Education

Resource kids, of whom seventy-five percent were boys. They were active students and many were frequent visitors to the assistant principal's office. Her students had read a scene from *Hamlet*, watched a video, and were now analyzing the main character's dilemma of jealousy, anger, and frustration with his life. What engaged her students was her ability to connect Hamlet's problems to their own daily lives. They felt connected with "this Hamlet character."

Read and Read

A teacher needs a strong grasp of the time period and the background information. A teacher needs the ability to sift through what's critical and what's not. He needs the capability to approach the problem from all angles, looking at it from the political/diplomatic, social, economic, and literary points of view. My philosophy is if it's not important, don't teach it. Otherwise, you're just going through the motions.

Mapping out a Teaching Rhythm

Rhythm is based on the objectives of the course and on a teacher's strengths. Rhythmic peaks represent a teacher's strengths in those course areas. I particularly enjoyed teaching about the 18th century Constitutional era in U.S. History. In addition, I gravitated to other constitutional issues throughout our history. The "Plotting the Peaks" graph on the following page is a self-analysis that helped me identify the holes in my own training. For example, I would focus my summer readings (narratives, biographies and autobiographies, and literature) on a period in U.S. History that I needed to better understand. I spent one summer learning about the latter half of the 19th century and became familiar with issues and players. In the classroom, we found similar issues and concerns that connected the 19th and 20th centuries. I wrote curriculum and lesson plans that would further engage students in understanding an era that was foreign to them.

In "Plotting the Peaks" shown below, there are eighteen issues that I identified as critical to a survey course in U.S. History. The percentages represent the depth of knowledge that I needed in order to teach an Advanced Placement course. The percentages also showed me what I needed to further study.

Establishing a Rubric for Assessment

Determine how and what learning will be measured. Rubrics are a measurement describing levels of achievement at pre-determined benchmarks. For example, the Advanced Placement essay questions are graded on five tiers of achievement. In addition, a teacher should utilize a variety of assessment tools to meet the diversity of learning styles. Immediate feedback is a motivator.

(a) Research based on complexity and depth.   (GREEN)

(b) Oral presentation and active member of the audience. (ORANGE)

(c) Time use in class and meeting deadlines.   (GOLD)

(d) Collaborative efforts and teamwork.   (BLUE)

(e) The final product—persuasive essay,   (ALL COLORS)
   visual display, etc.

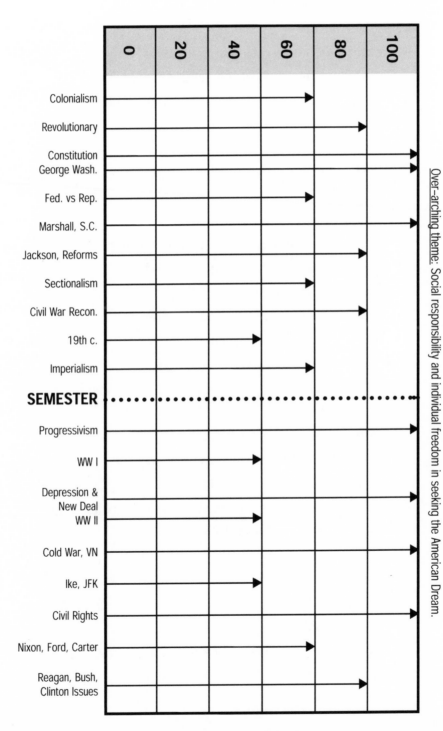

PLOTTING THE PEAKS

Over–arching theme: Social responsibility and individual freedom in seeking the American Dream.

Creating a Structure

—Create a timeline, a calendar.

—Set deadlines for each assignment; daily checks.

—Model what is expected, i.e., outline a muckraking
   project on the board.

—Involve whole class in discussions.

—Practice by picking an issue that is familiar, i.e., four-
   period day.

Come up with a hypothesis.

List where one could get information. For example,

   WAC (Washington Administrative Codes)

   District and school rules

Interviews—students, teachers, administrators, parents

Written resources—NASSP, books, journals, magazines

Come to a conclusion.

Discuss the visual displays that they could have included.

Continue to Monitor and Reinforce

—Check on students daily to help them stay focused.

—Keep on raising the bar (standards).

—Remember the refrain from the childhood book about the
   little train, "I think I can, I think I can..."

Get to Know the Kids

—Begin with a "recipe box" of 3x5 cards with information
   about the students.

—Honor a student's privacy by keeping the cards "for my
   eyes only."

—Let them know that they are special.

—Know their *True Colors* spectrum.

—Accentuate students' primary colors so they become experts ("professional") in a specific task. Start with their natural inclinations, which would most likely indicate their primary colors.

—Encourage and reach into their strengths in other colors so they are able to successfully take on a task by relying on each of their colors.

—Remember that it's all about them: what's best for the student, not what is best for us, the teachers.

EXAMPLE OF THE TYPE OF INFORMATION I NEEDED

FRONT

STUDENT'S NAME _____ GRADE_____

True Colors spectrum_____

Birthday_____

Advisor_____

Phone_____

Mother's name_____ Wk. Ph._____

Father's name_____ Wk. Ph._____

Student's favorite subject(s):_____

_____

Student's least favorite subject(s):_____

_____

BACK

Student's hobbies:_____

_____

_____

After graduation student plans to:_____

_____

_____

In ten years student wants to be:_____

_____

_____

Dates of contacts with student, parents:_____

_____

Helping Students Focus—Shifting a Stone Wall

Students, who are unfocused, have difficulty learning and retaining information. They need to honestly see themselves and gain a different perspective of their situation. I paint a scenario, with the student as the main player: I make believe that energy and time are finite commodities. Say a person has only one hundred units of energy and time to spend per day. If a student spends sixty units being angry, hostile, or frustrated, he will have only forty units to spend on learning, maintaining relationships, and perhaps a job, let alone units for esteem. Continuing with this example, I remind him that if he is doing well in my history class, he might be doing so with only twenty units of energy and time. Think of what he could do with forty or fifty or more? Finally, I ask him to assign the number of units for his "unfocused agenda." I have seen too many students spending seventy-five units on anger, revenge, and other destructive activities. They stonewall learning. By helping them visualize and analyze their energy and time units, they may begin to change their patterns of behavior.

It's About Empowerment and Growth

A poster, at the entrance of a bookstore near the Pike Place Market in Seattle, caught my attention. I don't know who authored it. It made me think of all the children whose paths I crossed in my thirty years in education.

To read is to empower
To empower is to write
To write is to influence
To influence is to change

Teachers can change the world. We have to believe within ourselves that what we are teaching is important and valuable to students. Learning builds the confidence and autonomy that empower students to take control of their own future. We have to have enough faith in them to let go and let them discover their own capacities and abilities to apply what we have taught them. This means pushing our own intellectual and emotional boundaries to become excellent. Without having experienced this process, how can we encourage students to increase their boundaries? The level of motivation in the classroom seems to be commensurate with the level of training a teacher receives, bolstered by the teacher's love for students. Motivation for teaching is grounded in a personal belief system.

I believe that:

- All kids want to become smarter.
- All children can learn.
- Every child has the potential to be good at something.
- The purpose of education is to help students gain knowledge, skills, and attitudes that will enable them to solve problems constructively and thus contribute to their own well-being and that of their society.

Chapter 9

A TEACHER: CRADLING THE SPIRIT

The Gatekeeper

Education is the gatekeeper. It opens doors to a person's dreams and goals. It makes the impossible seem possible. It brightens opportunities and allows one to seek fulfillment and happiness. It gives purpose to life.

On the flip side, ignorance alienates a person from his peers and from society. It blocks a person from feeling fulfilled and successful. It will likely bring harm to the person and to others.

If education is the gatekeeper for children, a teacher is the guide that lights the way. The only ticket required at the gate is the student's effort. Walking through the gate represents knowledge, skill, awareness, and purpose.

Teaching is a people business based on dynamic interactions and personal connections. It's about relationships. It's letting the Blue part of *True Colors* shine through. Teachers, who inspire, are artists. They not only create curriculum and encourage the development of talents, but also hold on to the sensitive spirit of a child. Part of a teacher's job is to protect the child's spirit.

In cradling the spirit, a teacher nurtures the dreams and hopes of a child. A teacher provides a safety net for children wherein they can take risks, try, fall, and try again until they succeed. During this sensitive process of learning, I figuratively hold up a mirror for them to see themselves: How they appear now and where they want to go. My goal is to have students develop confidence in themselves so they can hold up their own mirrors. Eventually, they will no longer need me.

Several people come to mind as I recall "cradlers of my spirit" during my growing years. I was fortunate to have loving parents and siblings. This is not always the case for a large number of students. For many, people at school are those whom they look to for the stability and love. Among these folks are teachers, administrators, counselors, librarians, and all the support staff, such as bus drivers, custodians, cooks, teachers' assistants, volunteers, and others who work with children. Their smiles and greetings can make a difference, particularly if a student is having a bad day. They can make him feel special. I am talking about fostering a positive school climate.

Laws can forcibly curb violence, but they may not change people. Replacing hatred with tolerance takes legislation, media support, and education. I believe education directs us toward a more peaceful world, promotes better relationships, and generally uplifts the whole of humanity. I have attempted to couch my teaching philosophy and practices in the following beliefs:

- Relationships are built on trust.
- Everyone should be treated with respect.
- Everyone wants to feel special.
- Everyone can grow and change.
- We are committed to the democratic principles of
    Equality and Equity

Justice and Fair Play

Unity and Diversity

Compromise and Consensus

Individualism and Social Responsibility

Dialogue and Public Forum

The purpose of schools now is not much different from the past. We still believe that students need to acquire basic knowledge and skills that will help them function successfully. We need to hold on to what is good, increase our knowledge and skills, and focus on creating a better world. I believe in idealism propelled by pragmatism.

Today the school population reflects the volatile, frenetic pace of a post-industrial society. We seem to be searching for a quick fix to our problems, which is often romanticized in the tabloids and other media. Values such as trust, hard work, discipline, loyalty, compromise, and excellence seem to be undermined by a materialistic, addictive subculture.

As problems multiply in disproportion to resources and solutions, many look to schools for a resolution. The expanding role of teachers and schools increases the tension by straining the schools' resources and energies. In a time when academic standards are being measured and tested in every state, the demands for non-academic responsibilities have quadrupled.

In many instances, the problems have paralyzed the learning process, and we question our faith and ability to educate everyone. I believe that a collaborative team of educators, students, and citizens can provide the best educational opportunities for every child. This mission is non-negotiable.

We have fought for a long time to establish public education for all children, regardless of intellectual, economic, emotional, and physical differences. Without an educated population, democracy will flounder and the whole of society will suffer. My thesis, that we are on a journey to create a better world order, can only be achieved through education.

I will not elaborate on the topic of the human spirit, because there are many experts who have written on its meaning. As it impacts the teacher-pupil relationship, I can only discuss what I have observed as a professional educator.

I find the human spirit to be perplexing, mysterious, and fascinating. On one hand the spirit is indomitable. The world can be falling apart and the spirit presses on. Hester in *The Scarlet Letter*, Richard Wright in *Black Boy*, and Anne Frank in her *Diary* are three examples of indomitable spirits. Our guest speakers from the World War II Holocaust humbled us with their tales of horror and survival, and we were awed by their grace and ability to turn a nightmare into a drive to improve humanity.

U.S. History and Psychology teacher, Roy Mainger, designed lessons centered around the Holocaust and people's will to survive. He raised the awareness of historical examples of injustice, inhumanity, and cruelty against those who were different. His unyielding passion for justice and kindness inspired others to see the world through the eyes of a compassionate person. His lessons created a climate in which students who were suffering their own private holocausts of abuse and neglect, could be heard. The human spirits continue to fight for survival in Southeast Asia, Africa, Eastern Europe, and other parts of the world.

Survivors of domestic upheavals also have strong spirits too. Two students from one of my 1982 classes come to mind. Being new to school and the community, Rebecca and Jamie, both 11th graders, bonded to each other immediately. They shared the common experience of being victims of abuse and neglect.

> Rebecca's current home was her fourteenth foster home in sixteen years. Bright, tough, and outspoken, she looked like she could stand up to anyone. But she also had a soft side that was sensitive and fragile. In the early 1980s the topics of domestic abuse, rape, and alcoholism were rarely discussed openly.
>
> There was a "no contact" order against her biological parents, who eventually immigrated to Canada. Rebecca's research paper on child abuse educated her peers and me about the depth of the problems, the lack of adequate legislation and support, and their effects on victims. During her senior year, she invited me to be her surrogate parent at a mother-daughter breakfast for graduating female seniors. I was honored. She had decided, by that time, to sue her parents.
>
> I did not hear from Rebecca for three years. Then, at the end of a school day, she appeared in my classroom. She was grinning, all grown up. She came to tell me that she was successful in her lawsuit and that she was happily married. She and her husband owned and operated a print shop. She was still optimistic about her future.
>
> Jamie, on the other hand, never returned to school for his senior year. No one knew what had become of him or his

family. He had had dreams of being a doctor, a profession quite in line with his talents. He was one of several siblings, but the only one enrolled in school. He said his mother was a prostitute in Reno and that they had lived in their car after they were evicted from their apartment. He said he engaged in illegal activities, but had never been arrested. He ached to live a "normal life." His research paper delved into teen homelessness and being forced to do whatever to survive. I don't know what became of him.

Like Jamie, Zack's whereabouts is unknown to me. My mind often reflects on him. I wonder if he survived his teen years. At sixteen he could have easily passed for twenty-one. Tall, athletic, piercing eyes, shaved head, serious, and verbal. Once in awhile, he would flash a great big smile and show off his beautiful set of teeth. When he came to Seattle from Chicago, he was an 11th grader by age, but a 10th grader by credits. He didn't like being in class with "those sopho-mores," whom he considered immature.

Zack was a loner and did not mingle much with other kids, who also kept their distance from him. They were sus-picious and fearful of this big kid from the Chicago streets. He carried himself confidently, liked being his own man, and did not hesitate to tell teachers how to teach a class. Teachers sent him to the assistant principal's office for insubordina-tion. According to Zack, the teachers were not doing their job in keeping their students on task.

Zack was insightful about what ought to be and liked challenging and arguing. Sometimes he would use my own argument to prove me wrong. We engaged in many conver-sations about power and control in the classroom, and I reminded him that there could only be one boss in the class-room—the teacher. He liked conversing in abstract terms. I supposed him to be a Green, whose esteem had been bruised over the years. Despite his reputation for being contrary and defiant, he was sixteen at heart, an orphan, and desperate for validation and respect.

When I disciplined and counseled Zack, I let him be cathartic. I listened to his tirade, his anger, and frustrations.

I found myself losing patience, because I was not getting through to him. Finally I said, leaning toward him and almost whispering, "Zack, I wish I had known you when you were a five-year-old." Raising his eyebrows as though he were anticipating an argument, he asked, "Why do you say that?" I replied, "Because I would have tried to stop whoever was hurting you."

There was an immediate change in his mood and tone. With tears in his eyes, he stared at me. For the first time, he was speechless. I couldn't fix his hurt, but I did hear and feel it. Maybe that was all he wanted. Our conversations became more meaningful from that point. Our discussions centered around his future, his dreams, his behavior. And curbing his temper.

Eventually his defiance and temper got him into trouble. He received several short suspensions for fights with students. Seven months after his arrival, he was expelled for assaulting a staff member. The staff member intervened to stop a fight between Zack and another student and was shoved up against the wall instead. I had counseled Zack over and over to keep his temper in check. I had expressed to him the regret I would feel, if one day I would have to sign papers for his expulsion from school. That day came; my signature was on his expulsion papers.

Zack had been falling through the cracks since his childhood. His experiences were far beyond his sixteen years. His father had been killed. He had inferred that he might have been a witness, but we never talked about it. His mother had remarried and there seemed to have been friction between Zack and his stepdad. At thirteen, he had a police record for assault. He joined gangs. His mother later died of a heart attack and he went to live with his aunt, and finally moved to Seattle to live with his brother, who had a stable job. After the expulsion, his brother relocated to Virginia and Zack went with him. I wished him luck in the new environment. Toward the end of the school year, I received a phone call from Zack from Virginia. No, he was not in school, but he was planning to return to Chicago and enroll in a school there. He needed his transcript. I never heard from him again. I hope an advocate stepped in to help him.

There are many other Zacks out there. They don't want to fail, but they do because there are not enough safety nets for them. They fall through the cracks. Despite the hardships they have endured, I am amazed at how spirited the Zacks, Rebeccas, and Jamies are. I am also respectful of the fragility of the human spirit. A harsh word or a harsh deed or hurtful comments and actions can send a sensitive individual into a tailspin of depression and dysfunction. Students seek approval from their teachers, even when they may exhibit all the traits of not wanting to be in class. It is said that we make five thousand decisions every day, and five of them impact someone forever. A teacher's words are powerful. They can contribute to students' confidence or chip away at their self-esteem.

Staying Healthy

Passionate teachers often do not have much of a life beyond school. Work and hobby become integrated, and other interests are postponed. In order for anyone to keep on giving, one has to stay in top shape mentally and physically.

Burnout is one of the primary reasons that talented teachers leave education. Kenneth J. Cooper of *The Washington Post* states, "About one of five teachers leaves the profession within three years of entering the classroom..." Virginia Edwards, editor of *Education Week*, says, "The best and brightest are most likely to leave."

Dealing with tougher students, added teaching responsibilities, and pressures from state and national testings are some of the reasons for teacher burnout. The weight of responsibilities becomes too burdensome and they leave the profession. The shortage of qualified teachers and administrators will be further deepened if there is no reversal in this trend.

In an attempt to educate the whole child, the teaching task has mushroomed to include academic, social, emotional, domestic and legal issues. Teachers' foremost complaint is they "can't get everything done," so they spend evenings and weekends "catching up." But they still do not have enough time to be super teachers. The pressure is unceasing and becoming increasingly oppressive. Thus, the wise teachers look after themselves first. They find balance in their lives, stay focused, and serve their community superbly. Trying one's best, while accepting one's limitations, is a rational goal.

Dr. Caroline Myss in *Anatomy of the Spirit* talks about becoming "spiritually centered" in the "high voltage pace" of lifestyle (p.10). By maintaining a healthy balance of diet, exercise, and mental and emotional attitude, we should become healthier (p.26). In keeping physically healthy, it is helpful to engage in daily physical activity. Going outdoors always provides a strong dose of energy. For the less athletic, walking, strolling, and gardening are good activities. Eating healthily provides the body and mind with the fuel to sustain energy. Stretching our intellectual faculties helps us become more knowledgeable about other disciplines and an expert in our own field. Maintaining healthy relationships buoys our own spirits so that we are operating from our Centers (*Dots*).

If a teacher is going to guide others, he must draw on his inner balance. One can't be a stranger to himself.

Choosing one's vehicle

My teaching vehicle was history. Studying history is one of my joys. It speaks to my dominant Gold and Green. I'm convinced that most people are born to love history, regardless of their *True Colors*. They like gossip, they enjoy intrigue and mystery, and they covet a good story. They are essentially curious about who did what to whom and when. History has many good stories. But the intrigue and excitement of history are often missing in the classroom.

"Ugh! I hate memorizing all those facts and dates," and "It's so-o boring" are students' comments about history, more than "I love it." I am specifically talking about United States History, taught in grades 5, 8, and 11. It is a Washington State requirement for graduation. So why so many negative vibes about history?

Studying history is like piecing together a giant puzzle: a person can finish one section at a time, comprehend that completed section, but can't quite see the whole picture. In making a puzzle, one must consider size, shape, texture, and color. Both learning history and making puzzles are similar in that one can approach a solution by various routes; one can begin anywhere, but the direction made has to be methodical and logical.

History, however, is more than a puzzle. A whole lot more. It's one of the best ways to understand self and others. It forces one to take a microscopic view of another person in another time frame. One asks: "Who did what to whom when?" and the most important question, "Why?" Whom did a decision impact? Are we still influenced by that decision today? By getting our noses in somebody else's problems and by coming to our own conclusion, we learn to weed through our own emotions, issues, problems and come to understand our needs, talents, motivations, and goals.

History allows us to find out about ourselves on someone else's turf. The process is the same, whether we deal with 19th century issues or our own personal issues. (1) Lay out all the details—the facts and dates; (2) sort out the details—examine, categorize, eliminate, save; (3) decide on a feasible, rational thesis or generalization based on the information at hand; (4) test the thesis from all possible angles and see if the generalization holds up; (5) gather more facts along the way; (6) hold on to the thesis or modify it according to further investigations; (7) do something about it.

School is both a reflection and an extension of the community. Our Washington students were encouraged to share their knowledge by actively participating in school and community services, such as peer tutoring, political campaigns, homeless shelters, and food banks.

I taught and advised several Political Conventions classes. A team of teachers and I trained students, grades 8-12, who role-played state delegates to a Mock Presidential Nominating

Convention in Portland, Oregon. The year-long preparation was sponsored by the Oregon Council for the Social Studies and the Beaverton School District. These events had been going on since the 1960s. In our first Convention, in 1972, our students played Democratic delegates from Tennessee; in 1980, they played Republican delegates from Massachusetts; and in 1984, they were Washington State Democrats. They became experts in every aspect of the election process, including working with the media, fundraising, debating, platforming, and working with candidates. Our students became resources to the Everett-Mukilteo community through speaking engagements and their participation in precinct, county, and state caucuses. A couple of students attended State Conventions, and one became a delegate to the National Convention. Their political savvy and sophistication touched the rest of the student body in dynamic ways. By spreading their political fever throughout the school and community, they sparked tremendous interest. Their depth of knowledge, skill, optimism, "can do" attitude, and camaraderie were lasting by-products.

Whether it is with our students, colleagues, family, or friends, we cannot lift another's spirit without lifting our own. This process is symbiotic. By lifting someone's spirit, we are often paid back in full. When our actions make someone else buoyant, we feel good.

Chapter 10

WATCHING THE MASTERS

What Does a Master Teacher Look Like?

We look to masters who set the standards on excellence (the *Dot*). The more renowned examples include Plato and Lao Tsu, as teachers and philosophers, Abraham Lincoln as a statesman and politician, Leonardo da Vinci, as the consummate artist, Mother Teresa, as a caregiver, and Jesse Owens, as an athlete who achieved greatness by transforming athletics into art. Historically, women have been overlooked, or they have been shut off from opportunities to seek the *Dot* in public ways.

There are masters among our teaching colleagues. They exemplify the best attributes of an artist. I recently attended a retirement party for three teachers who collectively have over ninety years of teaching experience. Having taught for some thirty years each is not as exceptional as being recognized as a Master Teacher. Their colleagues showered them with accolades, testimonials, and anecdotes.

What makes a teacher a Master Teacher? What do these three retirees have in common? When I see them, I perceive the brightness of the full spectrum of their *True Colors*, which is their strength.

One colleague commented on "how smart they are." They study and learn and consistently pursue scholarly answers to problems. Their knowledge of their respective specialty is extraordinary. They enjoy learning and knowing. They mastered their craft. Being scholars, they do not stop at defined departmental boundaries; their knowledge spans the disciplines. Their *Greenness* surfaces.

They are generous with their time and talents. They share. They mentor students, student teachers, new teachers, as well as fellow veteran teachers. They give and give—to their colleagues and most of all to their students and families. They care about the kids and their successes. They are gentle people with a lot of class. They never give up on reluctant learners. They will create new avenues to reach them. Their driving question is: "What can I do better to help these kids understand?" They are constantly trying to figure out what works. They stand apart from others by their originality in what and how they teach. They make connections with whom they come in contact. Their conversations are deep, substantial, and caring. They wear their *Blueness.*

They have the same persistent attitude whether they are planning a field trip, designing curriculum or working on a committee. They are individualistic, but at the same time, a team player. They have chaired or been a member of major committees. This combination of qualities has shaped the climate of their school. Their *Goldness* is reflected in their sense of responsibility, dependability, and concept of excellence.

Another trait they share is their broad interest in life's experiences, which expresses their *Orangeness*. Sharon Ruff, whose specialties are American Literature, creative writing, and

English language, is also an artist, an accomplished calligrapher and cartoonist. Her humor is evident in her cartoons and creative captions. In addition, she designs one-of-a-kind cards for all occasions—get well, birthdays, holidays. On occasion she makes her own paper. Even her grade book looks like an art piece. The platter of goodies, which she prepares for weekly departmental meetings are also works of art. Her artistry is evident in the interior decor of *Zella C.*, a classic, Prohibition Era wooden boat that she and her husband refurbished.

Sharon Ruff's grace and humanity set the tone in her classroom. Students attempt to emulate her actions and attitude. Her colleagues admire her. Sharon is most comfortable in her Blue mode and gets the biggest thrill when she observes her students' final products. Her *Blueness* sets the atmosphere, but her process is Gold. She relies on her *Goldness* to strive for success with all her students. She plans in great detail the day-to-day activities. Her students keep a daily journal and are aware of their responsibilities.

Encouraging students to undertake multi-media projects has become Sharon's trademark. The 1920s theme of "artistic expression of the time reflecting the change" talks about "breaking the rules" of a post-World War I society that fostered tradition and conservatism. Her students are assigned to research the 1920s, choose a specific topic, and apply it in a multi-media platform. They are to use sound (auditory appeal), text (similar to an advertising campaign), visualization (PowerPoint or Hyper Studio), and movement (animation). Sharon guides and monitors her students constantly. She is available to them before and after school, and even on weekends.

For their final evaluation, students must present their product to an audience, which includes at least three people from outside the classroom, such as someone from the community, another teacher, or an administrator. Students create their own invitations and thank you notes. They plan their fifteen-minute presentations. They have to cull the most important aspects of their research, compressing all they have learned into a few minutes.

One of Sharon's projects has been widely adopted. Sharon and Fran Sanford collaborated to produce children's literature by connecting high school students with first graders. Sharon and Fran have presented their lessons at numerous conferences throughout the Northwest. Over a two-month period in the fall, both groups of students come together four times. Unbeknownst to the first graders, the high school students are already preparing to write a book about their selected pupil. The high schoolers interview the first grader, get to know their likes and dislikes, their strengths and fears, and their families. Each child has two or three teenage partners.

In class, the high schoolers learn the elements of great children's literature. They study and discuss attributes of classic adult and children's literature. During the second meeting, the teens choose one of their favorite children's books. For the third visit, the first graders go to the high school to read their favorite stories to the teens. In the meantime, the high schoolers work hard to compose a story, create images, colorize, revise, edit, and re-edit. They have to keep in mind the detailed criteria established by the teachers. Each book is at least thirty pages long. The deadline is the week of the winter break, at which time the books are read and presented to the children. When the first graders find out that they are the heroes/heroines of the stories, they produce huge smiles, which are the greatest rewards for these teens. That look of surprise and delight is imprinted in the teens' memories. In addition to the academic value of this project, the attribute of sharing a most-treasured gift is learned. The teens give away a product that they have toiled over and spent hours perfecting to make a child happy.

One touching story is about a child whose early years had been tumultuous. He felt more secure after he moved in with his grandmother. But conditions were still difficult. For a while, the grandmother and child lived in a car. The teen's book to the child was the one meaningful gift he received that year for Christmas, and the whole book was about him. Grandmother was effusive in her thanks to the teachers and students for making her grandson feel so very special.

Many of those first graders are now in high school themselves, and they still know exactly where *their* book is on their bookshelf. They say they never forgot the experience. And that goes for the giver, too.

Steve Koepp, chairman of the science department, makes chemistry "so much fun," as one student commented. He is a favorite among many students. His enthusiasm is noised beyond his classroom walls. A colleague in the next room commented that he and his class often stop to listen to Mr. Koepp's lectures, because they were dynamic. Steve says he is a Primary Green, but he uses his colors to create a memorable experience for his kids.

Who would imagine that *The Pit and the Pendulum,* by Edgar Allan Poe, would be the highlight of a student's year in physics? By tying science to literature, Steve reads aloud Poe's story, but stops before the ending. Cries of "Then what happened? Finish the story, Mr. Koepp," echo across the room and down the hallway. There is always a scurry to get to the library to locate a copy of the book.

Steve challenges his students to figure out how many seconds the victim had to escape the pendulum. Students are at the school's stairwells, swinging ropes and estimating the arc's width. How long did Poe's character have to escape the torture?

Steve ignites the students' imaginations by letting them experience how science works and by seeing the relationship between nature and human conditions. His biggest thrill is the "ah-ha" moments. Their looks tell it all. His former students still remember after thirty years. His mission is "to enrich their lives on more than one level."

Steve lives his motto: "You can learn anything if you want to." That is true. He learned carpentry by volunteering as a helper to a contractor. Later, he built his own house. In 1977 he and his wife were a young couple without many financial resources. But, they had a lot of energy, determination, and faith in themselves. He studied furniture making, and his beautiful creations are still in his home. The couple wanted a piece of stained glass for their entry, so he learned the art, designed a piece for his home, and then taught his students during Mariner High School's mini-term. The physical activities he pursued were river rafting, mountain climbing, and water sports. Photography was his quietest hobby.

Ron Leonard did not begin his career as a teacher. His background was in rocket research and quality control. He was also, at one time, a plant manager of a plastics operation. His impressive list of former employers include Lockheed, Procter and Gamble, Hunt, and Polimar. He worked for ten years in the private sector, where his training in mathematics, chemistry, and physics was in great demand.

But, his heart was in teaching. He brings to the classroom his experience in management, teaming, and his passion for learning. He internalized the Model School truism: "Is it good for kids?" That became his measuring stick for what to do and not to do in the classroom. He is constantly figuring out what works, and if it doesn't work, why. He banks on his knowledge, experience, and originality to help kids understand the worlds of science, mathematics, and humanity.

Ron's philosophy of teaching is based on the three pillars:

Know your stuff.

Know who you're stuffing.

Stuff with grace and understanding

His integrity, humor, and passion are his assets. Outside the classroom, he is a wine connoisseur. His curiosity in the chemistry of wine-making led him to bottle his own brand. He knows grapes, chemistry, and business operations. He is an outdoorsman and takes advantage of the Puget Sound waters. Kayaking, boating, and crabbing are his favorite hobbies. For indoor sports, he and his wife are into round dancing. Ron seems to be a Primary Green with a strong second Orange.

Being a Master Teacher requires brains, heart, attitude, and originality. The blending of these ingredients is not an easy task. Sharon Ruff, Steve Koepp, and Ron Leonard truly leave examples of what a teacher can be. Not only have they been deemed Master Teachers by their local colleagues, but they also have been given that distinction by state and national organizations. I consider them to be the heavy hitters in education.

They leave behind a cadre of younger teachers who, they believe, will become Master Teachers. The arsenal of excellent teachers in their departments has been developed through their leadership and guidance over a long period.

In the early 1970s, Sharon Ruff, Steve Koepp, and Ron Leonard were all recruited by Principal Cliff Gillies to staff Mariner High School for the Model Schools project. What they remember about these early days—in spite of the turmoil that comes from trying something new without any blueprints—is the belief in and commitment to a dream to create a school that was "good for kids." Gillies's criterion for any innovation by a teacher was "Is it good for kids?" Simple. That attitude fostered thirty years ago is still alive today at Kamiak High School, under the leadership of Bill Sarvis. At both Mariner and Kamiak, the basic optimism is having faith in the teachers and empowering students. In their drive to do what was best for kids, Cliff Gillies and Bill Sarvis are admired by those who worked with them.

Other Masters

I like being surrounded by excellent teachers because they are inspirations for me to improve my craft. I've been fortunate to have been in the company of many masters. I remember Bob Tschirgi. He could mesmerize his audience with his stories of Greek gods and goddesses and medieval tales. His quick wit was phenomenal. John Orr, department chair in mathematics, made math fun for students. His ability to explain the complex in everyday language, and his diagrams and sketches on the overhead projector were magic to students. His humor and hearty laughter set a welcoming tone for his students, even those who had struggled with math.

Humor is a critical part of successful teaching. Like John Orr, Susan Davis's sense of humor opens her up to her students. She takes the fear out of Algebra II and Trigonometry, and students actually enjoy those tougher courses. Her passion for providing equal opportunity, for both students and staff, is remarkable. Her leadership in the Math, Engineering, and Science Achievement (M.E.S.A.), for example, encourages minority students of color, particularly African American, Hispanic, and Native American students, to enter these fields. Her message comes from her *Dot*. Another teacher, Jerry Morris, touches the *Dots* of his students in a pragmatic way. He increases his students' awareness of the law, the legal system, and teen responsibility. His classroom stretches beyond four walls and out into the community. His leadership in the Advanced Placement program in government is an extension of his commitment.

Beverly Forslof guided students to ask the big questions about life. She captivated her students with her vision of "what is important in life" and helped them articulate their own goals. She always began her class in September by having students design a coat of arms depicting who they are. The coat of arms was to describe a student's heritage, strengths, goals, and interests. Understanding and taking pride in themselves affected their performance and behavior in class. She was focused on both success in academics and in self-discovery. Her diagram of her "Quadrants," describing a hierarchy of learning, is still imprinted in the psyche of her students. They remember the "Quadrants" throughout their adulthood, fostering meaningful conversations. Beverly taught English and Psychology for thirty-four years and left a mark as an innovative leader and teacher of the International Baccalaureate program.

The first time I heard of TPR (Total Physical Response) was in the 1980s. I participated in a demonstration by foreign language teachers, Joy Abbey-Adams (French), Llyn Brickley (Spanish), and Steve Watkins (Russian). TPR is a method for teaching a foreign language that gets students to comprehend and apply that language. TPR is a highly interactive method of learning that allows one to learn a different language in a short time. The props are varied and imaginative. TPR is taught differently from the 1950s' and 1960s' textbook-driven, endless-recitation methods. TPR relies on multi-sensory cues and addresses all learning styles. Enrollment in the foreign language program has tripled.

Like the foreign language teachers, art duo Rudy Kovacevich (now retired) and Robert Stockton are legendary. They motivated students to create art of such caliber that it could have been displayed in galleries. Many of their students have actually gone on to study art and make their living as artists. Rudy and Robert embrace a wide view of art and art appreciation. Because of their conviction that every individual is an artist, they respect and treat each person as a precious learner. By modeling talent and character, they have demonstrated their *Dots* to help students visualize potential excellence. Art, at Rudy's and Robert's school, became one of the most sought-after classes.

John Hansen is the "kindest person," according to one student. Although Blue is not his primary *True Color,* his compassion for his students, particularly those who struggle with history, comes through. Academically, John knows his stuff (U.S. History). He heightens students' awareness and appreciation of the American culture so that they can solve personal and societal problems. By example, he demonstrates what a gentleman is in the classroom and on the athletic field. In 1991, he was named "Coach of the Year" by *The Everett Herald* after the spectacular state championship games in which his girls' softball team won the title. He lives what he preaches—integrity, responsibility, commitment, sportsmanship, compassion, and generosity. He walks his talk, as his students attest.

Bill Costello brings all his experiences into his senior English classes. Students are captivated by his stories, laugh at his anecdotes, and learn to connect their personal experiences to lessons in literature. His students do very well on AP and standardized tests. He is an intellectual. He is also an athlete, a coach, a world traveller, a serious Alaskan salmon fisherman during the summer months, and a genuine comic. He is one of the funniest persons I have known.

The positive relationship between Bill Costello and his students was evident in an April Fool's prank directed at him. His First Period class wanted to surprise him. At six o'clock in the morning, they moved all the desks, chairs, file cabinets and bookcases through the window in his classroom, and replicated everything outdoors. Imagine his surprise to find a totally empty classroom. Outside, his students were all seated and diligently working on their assignments and his TA had taken roll. He crawled through the window and began his lesson with a quote from Camus.

There are many, many masters who are not mentioned here. They are walking among us. My recommendation to teachers, especially the beginning teachers, is to look for models and follow in their shadow. Have meaningful conversations with them and let your own uniqueness blossom.

Chapter 11

Meaningful Conversations
Last a Lifetime

Meaningful conversations can take place anywhere, anytime. Imagine a meaningful conversation between two individuals face-to-face, or between two or more people through technology. Imagine an inner conversation with yourself, such as those that occur when you attend lectures, view television, or listen to the radio. Someone or something triggers the thinking process to cause you to analyze, synthesize, create, and talk to your inner self.

In Hawaii we call conversations "talking stories." Talk story is Hawaiian slang in pidgin-English for people engaging in friendly or heated conversations. Hawaiians tend to be talkative and sociable. "Come talk story" is an invitation to join in the conversation.

The Hawaiian heritage of oral history, sharing one's story with others, thus preserving it for future generations, is powerful. One author decided to transform oral into written history. A collection of stories, *Shaping Hawai'i: The Voices of Women*, written by Dr. Joyce Lebra, highlights women whose leadership and contributions made a difference in their communities. At the time of the interviews, the women were in their seventies, eighties, and nineties. Dr. Lebra writes as though the women

were talking to you. You could hear those pioneer women sharing their experiences. Each chapter focuses on one ethnic group
as they chronologically arrived in the islands. These groups
were the Hawaiian and part-Hawaiian, Chinese, Scottish-
English, Portuguese, Japanese, Okinawans, Puerto Ricans,
Koreans, and Filipinas.

In her chapter on the Japanese, the first story is told by
Teruko. My heart jumped when I recognized her as my sister-
in-law, the oldest of eight children in my husband's family. She
and her husband, Doc, were surrogate grandparents to our children. Doc passed away in 1993 and she died five years later
when she was in her late eighties. During Teruko's early days as
an elementary teacher, she began the first school for disabled
students on the island. Her students ranged from ages five
through thirteen. Many of them had never attended a "real"
school. Her compassion for the underdog was unwavering.

I knew Teruko when she was a community activist for
humanitarian and educational causes. What I remember most
clearly was her gift as a storyteller. Her father, a Buddhist
priest, told her to practice talking to a tree. She did. "According
to my father, there are yellow leaves and green leaves, and all
kinds of leaves. And they were the children. And they are
always moving. So he referred to the leaves as…children. And
this is the way I practiced." She shared her gift as a storyteller
long after she left teaching. She was a popular resource for
schools and community organizations throughout her lifetime.
My children vividly remember "Aunty's stories about the
olden days."

Talking stories in Hawaii is one form of communication. Teachers and students, and parents and children need to talk stories more often. Time is a precious commodity. Exchanging thoughts and feelings is best done in a one-on-one, face-to-face situation. But that is not always possible. A high school environment, for instance, is not conducive for such exchanges. Within the traditional schedule (55-minute class period) with thirty students, each student would receive less than two minutes a day for a private conversation with the teacher. Thus, before and after school, during lunch and prep period and evening phone calls seem to be the times when quality talks occur.

One of the topics regarding school reform is the lack of connection between a youngster and an adult. To correct this, innovations in structuring schools are being implemented. River Ridge High School, a new high school in the North Thurston School District in Washington, implemented such a structure. The school's goal of getting to know each student over a four-year period is key to their success. Certificated and classified staff members meet with small groups of students every day for seventeen minutes. They monitor the students' attendance, performance, and behavior before there are problems. Additionally, River Ridge is divided into four houses, each with about three hundred students and a core staff of certificated and classified educators. Students go to the main area for certain courses, such as physical education, laboratory science, and Home and Life. The school-within-a-school concept helps students connect to a school family.

A different concept of another new high school planned in the Arlington School District, also in Washington State, is being designed by architects. With the passage of the school bonds to replace the existing seventy-year-old high school buildings, the district is hoping to open the new school by 2003. The design of the school revolves around three pathways. The pathways are adaptations of the American College Testing (ACT) World of Work map, which further divides education into six pathways: Business Operations, Business Contact, Social Services, Arts, Science, and Technology. Since the ACT pathways have been a counseling tool, students and parents are already familiar with the concepts.

Three houses, or pathways (Science and Technology, Business and Social Services, Arts and Humanities) will represent the core of the new Arlington High School. Each house will have its own structure, character, and ambience. In this paradigm, traditional divisions and combinations of courses will be examined to fully integrate them into this new vision. Like River Ridge, Arlington will have an area for the fitness and wellness programs and a central common area for "a kid gathering spot." Such a student-friendly school will become a place where all sorts of meaningful conversations can flourish.

Another feature of the new school will be its built-in capability to expand in order to absorb a rapidly increasing student population. Arlington hopes to retain its small-town community and charm, in which people can talk to each other openly and, at the same time, move forward to successfully educate all its students.

Some schools have established advisor or mentoring programs, much like Mariner's Advisor-Advisee, to encourage meaningful conversations. Children who receive special attention gain confidence and esteem. Esteemed children do not exhibit negative attitudes and anti-social behaviors.

Secretary of Labor, Alexis Herman, stated in an ABC television interview (May 2, 2000) that the average teenager spends eighty minutes a day, including weekends, with his parents. The eighty minutes may not necessarily include meaningful conversations. She advocates the Family Leave Act, which will provide flexible work hours for parents to better fulfill their role as parents. By slightly altering the structure of the work place, her hope is to provide opportunities for quality family time.

As I stated before, time is a precious commodity. Teachers rely heavily on written communication. Although it does not replace one-on-one interaction, written exchanges can be effective. A case in point: my notations on student papers, "must revise here," were being ignored because students did not know what I meant by "revise." I found I had to show them. Revisions made on the computer and communication via the Internet facilitate the process. However, nothing truly replaces the personal touch in communicating.

The impact of a meaningful conversation lasts a lifetime, because it connects to our spirits and defines who we are and what we can become. The memories of such connections linger on, I believe, long after the physical part of us is gone. Teaching offers a unique opportunity to engage in meaningful conversations on a daily basis and make a difference in another's life.

One of Susan Kelliher's students commented that she spent more time in a day with Ms. Kelliher than she did in one week with her mother. The student sees her teacher almost three hours a day, as a pupil and as a Teacher's Assistant. Without doubt, both teacher and student impact each other significantly. Teachers have the power to communicate attitude, knowledge, and a process in thinking. Students have the power to motivate teachers to become more insightful about their profession.

Susan models a strong work ethic, dedication, understanding, and commitment. Her six-week lesson, "Reality Check: Are You Ready?", simulates a real-life situation in which students learn to live on their own. The primary purpose of the lesson is for students to become financially and emotionally independent. Superimposed over this real-life lesson is the practical application of *True Colors,* which helps them understand themselves, choose a compatible roommate, and communicate effectively with fellow employees and employers.

Again, teachers have a tremendous impact on their students. The impact of seven special teachers ripples through my thoughts today. I appreciate now who they were more than I did in my youth. They lifted me.

For example, I remember an elementary school cook named Mrs. Apo. Mrs. Apo made me, a scared first grader, feel special. She gave me a great big smile when she saw me coming with a penny clutched in my hand. She had a knack of making others feel special, too. Each morning, she prepared "Penny Breakfast" which turned out to be a variation of yesterday's leftover lunch.

Since Mrs. Apo and her assistant were the only employees in the kitchen, a crew of student helpers was scheduled to work with her on a rotation basis. When I became her helper, I discovered how tough and meticulous she was in the kitchen. Her pace was fast; she thrived on cleanliness; and she never quit working. She worked us hard and she always had a treat for us at the end of the day. Watching her creativity in the kitchen—throwing ingredients together to make something out of nothing—inspired me to also be innovative in the kitchen. Today, I enjoy making her "stone soup." She was a special lady.

Mrs. Osmanski was my 4th and 5th grade teacher in a tiny sugar plantation elementary school. She, like other teachers, lived in one of the teachers' cottages on the periphery of the school grounds. I thought she was very old, but, thinking back, she was probably only in her early fifties. She was from the mainland, but opened her arms to diverse cultures. She never looked down on us local kids—poor, barefooted, pidgin-English-speaking children from immigrant stock. That was important to us, and because our society was segregated, the only *haoles* (Caucasians) we knew were the plantation bosses. She kept asking me what I wanted to be when I grew up, and when I told her, she said I was capable. She was a prodder, a pusher for learning, and generous.

Before our Christmas break one year, we kids talked about what to give our teacher. Many planned to give bottles of cologne (because Mrs. Osmanski loved to smell sweet), or candy, or a knickknack. Not having much money, I made her two potholders from scrap material from my mother's sewing room. Mrs. Osmanski loved the potholders and placed an order for several more potholders for her friends. I don't recall what she paid me, but I do remember her delight and praise. She made me feel special.

I continued to correspond with her throughout my college years and long after. She retired and returned to live with her son and his family on the mainland. I visited her once in 1959. One Christmas, many years later, I didn't receive a card from her. Her son wrote to say that she had passed away.

Mrs. Osmanski didn't coddle kids and she was definitely not a hugger. But I remember her for appealing to my Green side and for her appreciating the very Gold culture that I came from. I recall her stories about life on the mainland, which was like hearing about a life in another dimension.

Miss Bloder was also from the mainland—New York. In 1949 I thought she was also old, but she was probably only in her forties or fifties. She taught science, which was my weakest subject. Science required thinking from another part of my brain. I loved instead math, history, and home economics. She took a liking to me because I tried so hard to understand science, biology, and chemistry. I learned to enjoy those subjects only because of her.

Miss Bloder made me feel special, too, by giving her time to make sure I learned well. She encouraged me all along the way. She valued knowledge, hard work, and discipline. The day before my graduation from the George Washington University, a special delivery box arrived and in it was a beautiful vanda orchid lei. We continued to correspond through Christmas cards each year until her death in 1988.

I thought Miss Crabbe was one of the most beautiful teachers at our high school. Her eyes always looked like she was smiling. She taught 11th grade United States History. I loved her and the subject. History became my favorite class. Miss Crabbe taught me new ways to look at history and to analyze evidence before making conclusions. She was open, and valued curiosity and questions. By pointing to inequities and accepting diversity, she was ahead of her time. In the 1950s, textbooks interpreted history with a skewed viewpoint. They were silent, for example, on the contributions of women, ethnic minorities, and common folks. Her special gift was her ability to tell stories. I loved listening to her stories about pioneers, women, presidents, and tycoons.

We corresponded throughout my college years and beyond; she was delighted that my education was pointing toward teaching history in a high school. She returned to California after her retirement and unfortunately we lost contact with each other.

Miss Matsui was an attractive, young teacher who taught Home Economics. In the 1940s and 1950s, the course included an introduction to sewing, cooking, baking, and etiquette. Unaccustomed to western-style table etiquette, I was fascinated with the formal table settings. What a surprise to learn that each item of silverware and dinnerware had a special function and a specific name! Just knowing that helped me be more comfortable in both Western or Eastern situations. I believe teaching this class was her first teaching job, and she seemed to enjoy it.

We students giggled as we watched the romance blossom between her and another teacher. We liked being in her class.

The three teachers, who impacted me most during my teen years, were women. Female high school teachers were in the minority in high schools in the 1950s. My most memorable conversations are connected to these three teachers.

In college, two teachers in particular deeply touched me. One helped me love history even more. Professor Merriman valued creativity and depth. He was passionate about his subject and made accounts of historical events memorable with enthusiasm, humor, and wit. One had to get to his classes early to get a good seat, because "drop-ins" came to listen to his lectures.

I took every one of his classes and began to feel like a historian. Because he made Diplomatic History so enticing, many of us seriously considered applying for a Foreign Service position at the State Department after our graduation. I began my Master's program in Diplomatic History and International Relations.

Professor Bolwell terrified me at first. His stature was small but his bark was loud. As Dean of the Graduate School, he ordinarily taught graduate students, but I was one of his naive sophomores taking his Introduction to American Literature to fulfill a graduation requirement. He used to say he taught one undergraduate course per year in order to keep his perspective on teaching.

Prior to earning his Ph.D. in American Literature, he had studied engineering and medicine. We students thought he knew everything. Our biggest complaint against him was his level of expectation. "Who does he think we are, grad students?" We felt he pushed us too hard. We resisted but he cajoled us into doing things his way. Whining was not an option. He was definitely the boss of the class. He never gave us answers to a problem. He would throw out a problem, teach us a process, and back off. He refused to spoon feed us. When our thinking was superficial and shallow, we heard his bark.

American Thoughts and Civilization was a new major that combined the disciplines of U.S. History and American Literature. Professor Bolwell was one of its originators. I loved the subjects, declared my major in ATC, and chose him as my teacher for two more years. His passion for teaching, thinking, and writing with consistency taught me to look at the big picture through history and literature and see their relationship in defining our American civilization.

Underneath his hard shell, Professor Bolwell was funny and generous. He often invited students to dine with him in restaurants. Conversations were always intellectual. He was sensitive to the fact that I was a poor working student on a scholarship. His confidence in my ability to pursue a doctorate in American Studies made me feel special and helped me to gain confidence in myself.

In 1978, seven years after I had begun teaching 11th grade Humanities (U.S. History/English/American Literature) at Mariner High School, I found myself recalling what Professor Bolwell had talked about. I wrote to him about my teaching, family, and life in the Northwest. It had been twenty-two years since my graduation from GWU and I doubted that he would remember me. I wanted to thank him and to tell him that I was applying the training of my major in American Thoughts and Civilization.

At eighty-seven years old, he had some medical problems, but he was still very sharp. He wrote:

> One of the real pleasures and rewards of a lifetime of teaching is to receive such a letter as you wrote me, and to know I have had some contribution invested in the life of another person.... I remember you.... You describe a full, rich life, and a busy one, with your children and your teaching. I hope you receive the thrill of some letters like yours to me, from some of your own students. Thank you cordially for writing to me, and giving much pleasure to an old man.

He taught me to take risks in being creative in thinking and writing and in designing a research project. He challenged his students to assume a scholarly attitude toward learning. I, too, learned to bark at my students, "Think, think, think."

Professor Bolwell taught me to see the interrelationships between the academic disciplines of history, literature, science, mathematics, languages, and technology. Some of my greatest conversations with myself came through the media—James Burke's *The Day the Universe Changed* series, Joseph Campbell's *The Power of Myth* series, and Bill Moyer's ties to Campbell and programs on wellness and health. I have watched and listened to these over and over. I incorporated them into my curriculum and teaching style. I cannot look at teaching today without seeing a larger picture of human endeavor.

And what should a person endeavor to do? I certainly don't have all the answers or a sure-proof formula, but I can point to some common needs: to find happiness, to be loved, to be special, to fit in, to be able to fulfill dreams, and to be able to make a difference. A person of esteem helps himself and others to get ahead emotionally and intellectually. There is no room for racism, hatred, ridicule, or put-downs. Further, a person of esteem need not fluff his ego or tell the world how great he is—what I call the "Wonderfulness of Me" syndrome. A person of esteem is comfortable with himself and makes others feel comfortable in his presence.

No matter how complex and technologically sophisticated we become, our need to connect with each other is kneaded into the ingredients of growth and development. I have had decades of meaningful conversations, beginning in the sugar plantation village, which no longer exists, to today as a retiree who is involved with *True Colors*. I still run around barefooted, but I do it now by choice. I have learned that each of us finds our own commonality and differences, as well as our humanity, through recognizing our *Dots*. We shape our behavior from the *Dot*. That makes us all extra special.

READINGS

Boyer, Ernest L. *High School: A Report on Secondary Education in America*. NY: Harper & Row Publishers, 1983.

Boyer, Ernest L. *The Basic School: A Community for Learning.* Princeton, NJ: The Carnegie Foundation for the Advancement of Learning, 1995.

Campbell, Joseph. *An Open Life*. N.Y.: Harper & Row, Pub., 1989.

Campbell, Joseph. *The Power of Myth*. N.Y.: Doubleday, 1988.

Chopra, Deepak. *The Seven Spiritual Laws of Success*. San Rafael, CA: Amber-Allen Publishing & New World Library, 1994.

Chopra, Deepak, *The Seven Spiritual Laws of Success for Parents*. London: Rider, 1997.

Conway, Jill Ker. *True North*. NY: Vintage Books, 1994.

His Holiness The Dalai Lama and Howard C. Cutler, M.D. *The Art of Happiness: A Handbook for Living*. USA: Compass Press, 1998

de Chardin, Teilhard. *The Phenomenon of Man*. NY: Harper Torchbooks, 1959.

Devine, John and Cliff Gillies. *Victory Beyond the Scoreboard*. Wilsonville, OR: BookPartners, Inc., 1997.

Gardner, Howard. *Frames of Mind: Theory of Multiple Intelligences*. N.Y.: Basic Books, Inc., 1983.

Gillies, Cliff. *The Sports Management Journal for Families, Coaches and Kids*. Wilsonville, OR: BookPartners, Inc., 1999.

Gray, John. *Men are from Mars, Women are from Venus*. NY: Harper-Collins Publishers, 1992.

Gunnels-Perry, Sherryl. *What in the World Is Going On? Understanding, Impacting, and Going Beyond Education Reform*. Redmond, WA: Concept Graphics & Publishing, 1998.

Hall, Calvin S. and Vernon J. Nordby. *A Primer of Jungian Psychology*. NY: Penguin Books, 1973.

Hirsch, Jr., E.D. *The Schools We Need and Why We Don't Have Them*. N.Y.: Doubleday, 1996.

Huber-Bowen, Tonya. *Teaching in the Diverse Classroom: Learner-Centered Activities That Work*. Bloomington, IN: National Educational Service, 1993.

Jenson, William, Ginger Rhodes, H. Kenton Reavis. *The Tough Kid Tool Box*. Boston: Sopris West, 1994-96.

Kalil, Carolyn. *Follow Your True Colors to the Work You Love*. Wilsonville, OR: BookPartners, 1998.

Katz, Lawrence C. and Manning Rubin. *Keep Your Brain Alive*. N.Y.: Workman Publishing Co., 1999.

Keirsey, David. *Please Understand Me: Temperament, Character, Intelligence*. Prometheus Nemesis Book Co., 1998.

Krovetz, Martin L. *Fostering Resiliency: Expecting All Students to Use Their Minds and Hearts Well*. Thousand Oaks, CA: A Sage Publications Co., 1999.

"Kuder Career Search." Adel, IA: National Career Assessment Services, Inc. www.kuder.com

Kuhn, Betty. *When Mom Moves In*. Wilsonville, OR: BookPartners, Inc., 1999.

Lebra, Joyce C. *Shaping Hawai'i: The Voices of Women*. Honolulu: Goodale Publishing, 2nd edition, 1999.

Moore, Robert and Douglas Gillette. *King Warrior Magician Lover: Rediscovering the Archetypes of the Mature Masculine*. San Francisco: Harper, 1990.

Myss, Caroline. *Anatomy of the Spirit*. NY: Crown Publishers, Inc., 1996.

National Association of Secondary School Principals. *Breaking Ranks: Changing an American Institution*. Reston, VA: NASSP, 1996.

Palmer, Park J. *The Courage to Teach: Exploring the Inner Landscape of a Teacher's Life*. San Francisco: Jossey-Bass Publishers, 1998.

Report of the Superintendent's Middle Grade Task Force. *Caught in the Middle: Educational Reform for Young Adolescents in California Public Schools*. California Department of Education, 1987.

Robbins, Anthony. *Awaken the Giant Within*. NY: Summit Books, 1991.

Schurr, Sandra L. *Prescriptions for Success in Heterogeneous Classroom*. U. of So. Florida: National Middle School Association, 1995.

Sergiovanni, Thomas J. *Leadership for the Schoolhouse*. San Francisco: Jossey-Bass Publishers, 1996.

Sizer, Theodore. *Horace's School: Redesigning the American High School*. Boston: Houghton Mifflin, Co., 1992.

Sizer, Theodore and Nancy Faust Sizer. *The Students Are Watching*. Boston, Beacon Press, 1999.

Suzuki, Shunryu. *Zen Mind, Beginner's Mind*. New York: Weatherhill, 1981.

Toffler, Alvin. *The Third Wave*. NY: Bantam Books, 1980.

Toffler, Alvin. *Power Shift*. NY: Bantam Books, 1990.

Toffler, Alvin and Heidi. *Creating a New Civilization.* Atlanta, GA: Turner Publishing, Inc., 1995.

Wong, Harry K. and Rosemary T. *The First Days of School.* Mountain View, CA: Harry K. Wong Publications, Inc., 1998.

Zukav, Gary. *The Seat of the Soul.* New York: Simon and Schuster, Fireside Edition, 1990.

True Colors Publications, Riverside, CA: True Colors and Educational Services International.
- *Action and Communication Guide.*
- *The Corporate Communication Guide.*
- *The Corporate Communication Guide: An Effective Performance Tool for the Workplace* by Fred Leafgren and Joseph Sullivan.
- *Keys to Successful Teaching.*
- *Leadership, Management and Career Development for Corporations and Organizations,* Facilitators Guide.
- *Teacher's Guide for Lesson Plans.*
- *Welcome to True Colors Communicator.*

About True Colors

Our vision at True Colors is to foster positive, healthy, productive communities whose successes flow from the natural dedication of each person. Our powerful, customized "edutainment" workshops, books, workbooks, videos, live shows and events have empowered millions of people during the past twenty years and helped to realize this vision.

Listed below are some of the True Colors resources people across the country are turning to for improved communication in their personal and professional lives.

Also available from True Colors:

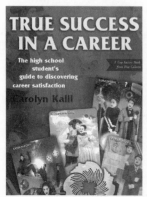

True Success in a Career
ISBN 1-893320-24-3

Written specifically for today's teens, **True Success in a Career** introduces high school students to the True Colors process and guides them toward careers that fit with who they are. Author Carolyn Kalil leads students through a journey of self-discovery to help them gain a better understanding of their natural strengths and identify careers in which they will find true satisfaction. 110 pages.

TCB-030 . . . . **$22.95***

Showing Our True Colors
ISBN 1-893320-23-5

Filled with easy-to-use tools for personal growth, this delightfully illustrated book by communication expert Mary Miscisin uncovers the power of the True Colors process. You will discover the characteristics behind each of the four True Colors, as well as tips for understanding, appreciating, and relating to each Color style. Its simple format, charming anecdotes, and convenient reference lists make **Showing Our True Colors** a fun and easy read. And the end result will be a celebration of the uniqueness in yourself and others. 242 pages.

TCB-020 . . . . **$19.95***

More creative resources from True Colors . . .

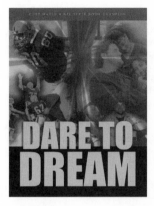

Dare to Dream
ISBN 1-893320-21-9

Super Bowl champ Curt Marsh challenges readers to dig deep and pursue their dreams, whatever their circumstances. Curt talks about the physical and emotional pain he endured when a football injury led to the amputation of his right foot and ankle. And he shares many of the life lessons that have inspired him to rise above his challenges and pursue his passions—including the True Colors process. **Dare to Dream** will inspire you to embrace change and diversity, discover true toughness, set goals and develop plans to achieve them, and much more! 122 pages.

TCB-010 . . . . **$19.95***

True Parenting
ISBN 1-893320-25-1

Author Kathleen Hayward guides parents through the True Colors process to determine the Color Spectrum of each family member and the family as a whole. Filled with fun activities for the entire family, **True Parenting** helps develop improved parenting skills, greater communication in the home, and more meaningful family relationships.

TCB-040 . . . . **$18.95***

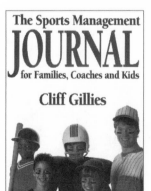

The Sports Management Journal
ISBN 1-885221-97-5

The Sports Management Journal is an easy-to-use workbook written specifically for school coaches and parents of children in sports. Author Cliff Gillies presents tear-out exercises to copy and use in daily coaching and parenting. You'll also find a proven design for coach-parent teaming, games for teaching respectful communication, charts for athletic achievement and improvement, the True Colors personality assessment system and cards, and much more! 179 pages.

TCB-061 . . . . **$14.95***

Action & Communication Guide - for Teachers and Parents

Our popular **Action & Communication Guide** will help identify the "personality" of your classroom and provide effective ways to help you better relate to each student. Features a durable binder and four "colorized" sections—one for each personality type. 88 pages chock full of valuable insight for creating a stimulating classroom environment, motivating learning and achievement, gaining cooperation and more!

TCP230 . . . . **$34.95***

TCP225-C (Without Binder). **$29.95***

* **Plus shipping and handling**

To order additional copies of

Meaningful Conversations or

any of these True Colors products,

please contact us at:

True Colors, Inc.

12395 Doherty Street,
Riverside, California 92503

Telephone: (800) 422-4686 or (909) 371-3901
Facsimile (909) 371-1701

E-Mail: info@truecolors.org

Web Site: www.truecolors.org